Other books by the late
I R V I N G   C H E R N E V :

THE 1000 BEST SHORT GAMES OF CHESS
INVITATION TO CHESS
LOGICAL CHESS, MOVE BY MOVE
THE MOST INSTRUCTIVE GAMES OF CHESS EVER PLAYED
WINNING CHESS
CAPABLANCA'S BEST CHESS ENDINGS: 60 COMPLETE GAMES
PRACTICAL CHESS ENDINGS
WINNING CHESS TRAPS
WONDERS AND CURIOSITIES OF CHESS

200

BRILLIANT
ENDGAMES

IRVING CHERNEV

with a Preface by
Bruce Pandolfini,
NATIONAL MASTER
and an Introduction by
Adam Hart-Davis

A   FIRESIDE   BOOK
Published by Simon & Schuster Inc.
New York   London   Toronto   Sydney   Tokyo

Fireside
Simon & Schuster Building
Rockefeller Center
1230 Avenue of the Americas
New York, New York 10020

Manufactured in the United States of America

10   9   8   7   6   5   4   3   2   1

Library of Congress Cataloging in Publication Data

Chernev, Irving
    200 brilliant endgames / Irving Chernev ; with a preface by Bruce
Pandolfini and an introduction by Adam Hart-Davis.
        p.   cm.
    "A Fireside book."
    Includes index.
    1. Chess—End games.   2. Chess—Collections of games.   I. Title.
II. Title: Two hundred brilliant endgames.
GV1450.7.C49   1989
794.1'24—dc19   89-31130
                                                                                    CIP

ISBN 0-671-67284-3

PREFACE

If there were prizewinning chess authors, Irving Chernev would surely be one of them. As it is, he is merely one of the most successful chess writers of all time. Not even Fred Reinfeld, his renowned contemporary who produced more than 200 different titles, sold more copies. The best of Irving Chernev's books are timeless and continue to sell well years after his death.

A music teacher by profession, Irving invested his writing with beauty, harmony, and perfection. It sparkles when he discusses inspiring moves and combinations, layering his analysis with pithy and insightful observations. Chernev never burdens the reader with too much commentary. He provides just enough to highlight key moves.

This was the style he used in the 1930s when writing his "Chessboard Magic" articles for *Chess Review,* as one of the initial contributors. Terse maxims, punctuated statements, brilliant moves were the basis of this regular column of classic endgame studies. He later grouped 160 into a stunning book with the same title as the column.

When Chernev died in 1981, chess lovers mourned. There would be no more revelatory books à la Chernev. But luckily, this was jumping the gun a bit. Among his final papers was one more treasurable book: a collection of impeccable endgame studies perhaps even surpassing those of his *Chessboard Magic.* Here they are in *200 Brilliant Endgames,* thanks to the perseverance of Irving's wife, Selma, and the efforts of Adam Hart-Davis and his son, Jason, who together put the finishing touches on the manuscript.

And what a final book Irving Chernev has given us! It contains 200 of the most brilliant ending combinations ever created by the game's great composers. Troitzky, Réti, Kasparyan, Benko, Kubbel, Rinck, Grigoriev, and many others are here for your enjoyment and pleasure, arranged in alphabetical order according to composer, unlike any other similar compilation. With this arrangement you can turn to your favorites immediately, though first wading through the entire collection is worth the excursion.

Each problem in *200 Brilliant Endgames* is introduced with a cue, such as "White to play and win." Every example includes the composer's name, the date of its original publication if available, a clear diagram with an algebraic grid, and the winning variation presented columnarly in algebraic notation. Only necessary analysis is provided, thus not interfering with your recreation and the flow of moves.

Some chess writers load on intricate variations that make reading a chore. But Chernev was an accomplished writer who said more by saying less. In three or four words, he gives the essence of an example, and that's "the point," to borrow one of his familiar expressions. In this final Chernev book, the master has bequeathed us a gem—200 gems, in fact. I know you'll enjoy them.

BRUCE PANDOLFINI

INTRODUCTION

Irving Chernev was born in Russia in January 1900. He enjoyed having such an easily remembered birthday; he never had any trouble filling in forms, or working out his age. He learned to play chess when he was twelve, and apart from his charming wife, Selma, and his books, and music, and food, chess was his only true love for almost seventy years. He died of cancer in September 1981.

Irving never claimed to be a great chessplayer, but he was devoted to the game, and for many years he wrote a chess column without pay because he wanted to share his enthusiasm with the rest of the world. Eventually he was persuaded to write a book, *Invitation to Chess*, with Kenneth Harkness, which became one of the most successful of all chess primers. After that he never looked back. He wrote some twenty books, including my favorite, *Logical Chess, Move by Move* (1957). It's simple, and sometimes naive, but also one of the best chess books ever written.

I edited three of Irving's books before this one. I know how much time, care, patience, and love he put into them. The typing was immaculate, the diagrams were beautifully laid out, and every word was chosen with care.

Irving was raised in suburban New York, and worked in the paper industry. When he retired, he and Selma moved to San Francisco. They settled in an apartment near Scot's, which was to become their favorite restaurant in a city famous for its seafood. Almost the only things that tempted them away were trips to London and Paris, where they stoked up on theater and *haute cuisine;* Irving was a gourmet, not only of food and of chess, but of life itself. I have met many chessplayers and many chess writers, but none of them has had the same sort of infectious enthusiasm for having fun. His letters were alive with humor; jokes and anecdotes crackled from the tightly packed typewriting on the smart cream paper.

He once went to a wedding in Las Vegas, where he had a successful battle with the one-armed bandits: "I managed to wrest $900 from their clutches. Of course I had to invest some $300 to do so, but I prefer to regard it as a clean profit of 900 smackers."

Early in 1978 he wrote to me in great excitement that he had lured Tigran Petrosian to his apartment for lunch. He had previously met five world champions—Capablanca, Alekhine, Lasker, Fischer, and Botvinnik.

Even when he was seriously ill with cancer his letters were full of fun. This was how he described one discharge from hospital:

> I was ready to leave at twelve when I reminded myself that I had already ordered lunch and dinner for that day; so I might as well eat lunch before leaving—or so I thought. When the boy came up with the luncheon tray, I asked him to cancel the dinner order, as I was leaving immediately after lunch. "Don't touch the lunch," was his reply. "If you do, it will cost you $265"—the charge for a day's stay. And as this was considerably more than I had ever paid at Maxim's, I decided to forgo the lunch, even though the main course was macaroni and cheese.

I enjoyed Irving's irreverence. Among his large chess library, his favorite book was Dr. Siegbert Tarrasch's heavy volume *Dreihundert Schachpartien* ("Three Hundred Chess Games"). He had read this so many times that it fell apart; accordingly, he took it to a local bookbinder and asked him to bind it in black leather. Then came the question of what should go on the spine. "Gold blocking," said Irving. But surely, said the binder, you don't want all that German stuff? "No," said Irving, "just put 'Holy Bible.'"

I met Irving only three or four times, mostly in London, and once in San Francisco. I used to look forward immensely to seeing him again: to the good food, the wine, and the conversation. Irving always produced a pocketful of newspaper clippings, an earful of anecdotes, and a battered leather wallet set with pieces designed by Marcel Duchamp, on which he would show me a couple of stunning positions. Once we played a game somewhere in the middle of dinner, but I can't remember who won.

Irving didn't really need to win. For most chessplayers, winning is what chess is all about. For Irving, however, the game itself was what mattered. He didn't want to beat anyone; he wanted to show everyone just how beautiful chess can be. Turn the pages of this, his final book, and you will see.

ADAM HART-DAVIS

EDITOR'S NOTE

Irving Chernev finished collecting the material for this book shortly before he died in 1981. He had written the notes and put the games roughly in order. Unfortunately he left the text in descriptive notation. Worse, it was in manuscript. Irving would have been the first to admit that his handwriting was imperfect—indeed, it has baffled cryptographers for years. All the old pungent wit is here—our favorite is the note after White's 5th move in Ending 64—and we have done our best to render it faithfully into algebraic notation and legibility. We've probably made mistakes—sorry—but we hope you enjoy these endings as much as we have.

ADAM HART-DAVIS
JASON HART-DAVIS
September 1989

Afansiev, Duizov, 1967

White to play and win

The obvious first move, 1 g4 +, winning the Rook, would be made by ninety-nine out of a hundred players. This powerful move fails! After 1 g4 + Kg6! 2 gxh5 + Kh7 3 Bc3 (or anywhere else) a1 = Q 4 Bxal, Black gets his draw by stalemate!

The right way:

1   Kf7

Now the threat of 2 g4 + is acute.

1   ...   Rh1

Certainly not 1 . . . Rg5 2e4 mate.

2	e4 +	Kg5
3	Bf6 +	Kh5
4	g4 mate	

A brilliant ending.

Afansiev, Duizov, 1969

White to play and draw

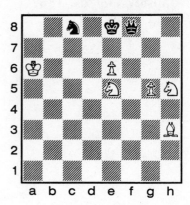

Quiet moves can be as forceful as moves that smite, as we see here.

1 Nf6 +   **Kd8**

Not 1 . . . Ke7, when 2 Ng6 + wins the Queen.

2 e7 + !   **Nxe7**

Forced, since capturing with King or Queen loses to a Knight fork.

3 Kb7!

Quiet, but effective.

3 . . .   **Qg7**

The only possible reply; the King may not move, the Knight dare not, since 4 Nc6 mate would follow, while the Queen has no other safe move.

4 Kb8!

White is content to wait or repeat moves.

4 . . .   **Qf8**

The Queen (alas!) has no other safe square open.

5 Kb7
        Drawn.

White's King quietly forces a draw by repetition of position.

Afansiev, Duizov, 1970

White to play and draw

Despite his precarious situation—a Rook under attack, and an adverse Pawn rushing down to become a Queen—White draws by an enchanting little combination.

1   Rxg6

Attacks the Bishop, and threatens 2 Rf6 +, winning the dangerous Pawn.

1   ...   Bg7 +

A clever, surprising resource.

2	**Rxg7**	**f2**
3	**e6**	**f1 = Q**

Or 3 . . . dxe6 4 Rg8 + Kf7 5 Rg7 + Kf6 6 Kg8, and the threat of 7 Rf7 + is decisive.

4	**Rf7 +**	**Qxf7**
5	**e7 +**	**any Stalemate.**

Apschenek, 1933

White to play and win

Black's King suffers from being hemmed in by his own army.

1	Re1	b1 = Q
2	Rxb1	Bxb1
3	e7	a2

On 3 . . . Bg6 instead to stop the Pawn, the reply 4 Be3 mate would be embarrassing.

4	Be3 +	g5

Forced, since 4 . . . Kg6 lets White promote to a Queen with check.

5	Bd4	

Restrains Black's a-Pawn, and threatens to Queen his own passed Pawn.

5	. . .	Bg6
6	Bg7 mate!	

The unfortunate King has no egress!

ENDING 5

Babic, 1901
White to play and draw

Exact timing characterizes this study.

1 Be5!

A sacrifice that must be accepted.

1 ...   Bxe5

On 1 . . . d4 instead, there follows 2 Bxd4 Bxd4 3 Kd5 b2 4 Kxd4 b1 = Q 5 Be4 + and the Queen falls.

2 Kxd5   Kf5

No better is 2 . . . Bf6 3 Ke6 and White controls the square e4 with his Bishop.

3 Bc6   b2
4 Ba4   b1 = Q
5 Bc2 +   Qxc2
        Stalemate.

ENDING 6

Badaj, 1967

White to play and draw

Skillful maneuvering by White's King enables him to escape from what seems certain loss.

1	Ke4	Nh4

If Black tries 1 . . . Nxh2 instead, there follows 2 Kxf4 Rg4+ 3 Kf5 Rxa4 4 Nxh2 and the position is drawn.

Or if 1 . . . Rg1 2 Kxf4 Rxf1 3 Bb5 Rf2 4 Kg3 Rb2 5 Bd3+ followed by 6 Kxf3 and draws.

2	Kxf4	Rf5+
3	Kg4	Rxf1
4	Bc2+	

Not at once 4 Kxh4, since the reply 4 . . . Rf4+ wins the Bishop.

4	. . .	Ng6
5	Kh5	Rf6
6	h4	Kg7
7	Bxg6!	Rxg6

Stalemate.

Belokon, 1968, First Prize

White to play and win

White ends this with a checkmate as exquisite as any you'll ever see. Both White Rooks are threatened, so he must attack immediately.

1	Rd5 +	Bf5

If 1 . . . Kh6, 2 Rxg4, all three of Black's pieces are in danger.

2 Rg1

Better than 2 Rxf5 + Kg6.

2	. . .	Ne7
3	fxg4 +	Kh6
4	Rd8	Bh7
5	Rxh8	Ng8

Shuts in the Rook and threatens to remove it by 6 . . . Kg7.

6	g5 +	Kg7
7	g6	

Now if 7 . . . Bxg6 8 Rxg8 + Kxg8 9 Rxg6 + wins at once.

7	. . .	Kxh8
8	g7 mate	

An elegant *coup-de-grâce*.

ENDING *8*

Bent

White to play and draw

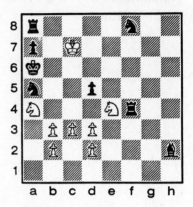

After seven moves, White has given away a Knight and all five Pawns—as fast as Black can take them—to force a clever draw by stalemate.

1	Nac5 +	Kb5
2	Nd6 +	Kxc5
3	b4 +	Rxb4
4	d4 +	Rxd4
5	b4 +	Rxb4
6	d4 +	Rxd4
7	cxd4 +	Kxd4

Stalemate.

Neither the King nor the pinned Knight may move.

A simple but pleasing endgame.

ENDING 9

Bent, 1967

White to play and win

Mr. Bent, England's leading composer of chess endings, provides a treat with this rare and beautiful finish.

1   Kf2

With the powerful threat of 2 Nf1—mate on the move.

1   . . .   Rxe4

If instead 1 . . . Rxg5, then 2 Nf3 + Kh3 3 Nxg5 + Kh4 4 Bxe7 wins.

2   Ndf3 +   Kh1
3   Nxe4

Again threatening mate on the move.

3   . . .   Nf5
4   Nc5!
     White wins.

Black is curiously helpless. His King may not move, and neither his Knight nor his Bishop can move without being instantly captured.

Bent, 1970

White to play and win

Underpromotion is the key to a win, whereas promoting to a Queen could meet with a startling reply. An original study by a great English composer.

1	Qc8+	Bg8
2	Qh3+	

But not the hasty 2 f7 when 2 . . . Qe7+ followed by 3 . . . Qxf7 removes all danger.

2	...	Qh6

On 2 . . . Bh7 instead, White wins by 3 fxg7+, since if Black saves his Queen by 3 . . . Kg8 then 4 Qe6 is mate.

3	Qxh6+	gxh6
4	f7+	Kh7
5	f8=N mate	

White could ruin everything (as Roycroft points out) by playing 5 f8=Q, when Black turns the tables by replying 5 . . . Nc2 mate.

Bernhardt, 1961
White to play and draw

White can avert the threat of 1 . . . Bd5 mate on the move only by generously sacrificing everything he owns.

1	b3!	Bxb3
2	c4	Bxc4
3	g8 = Q +	Bxg8

The Pawn sacrifices are reminiscent of Atalanta's ruse, where Milanion overcame Atalanta's swiftness of foot by tempting her with three golden apples that he threw in her path.

4	Nf7!	Bh7

Obviously 4 . . . Bxf7 is stalemate.

5	Ng5!	Bf5
6	Nf3	

Threatens to draw by taking the Pawn.

6	. . .	Be4
	Stalemate.	

Birnov, 1970

White to play and win

A simple, straightforward position—yet it requires care!

1 Ke2!

The plausible 1 f5 fails after 1 . . . a5 2 f6 a4 3 f7 a3 4 f8 = Q a2 5 Qa3 + Kb1, and the position is a book draw.

1	. . .	a5
2	Kd3	Kb2

On 2 . . . a4, 3 Kc3 wins easily.

3	f5	a4
4	f6	a3
5	f7	a2
6	f8 = Q	a1 = Q
7	Qb4 +	Kc1

On 7 . . . Ka2, 8 Kc2 forces mate.

8	Qd2 +	Kb1
9	Qc2 mate	

ENDING *13*

Birnov, 1947

White to play and win

White lets the Pawn become a Queen with check, but his gallant Knight saves the day!

The plausible 1 Rg1 fails after 1 . . . Kb7 and Black draws easily. The proper procedure is:

| 1 | **Rg7+** | **Kb6** |
| 2 | **a8 = N+** | **Ka6** |

Of course not 2 . . . Kc6, when 3 Rc7 is mate.

| 3 | **Nc7+** | **Ka5** |

On 3 . . . Kb7, 4 Ne6+ Kb6 5 Rg1 followed by 6 Rc1 wins the dangerous Pawn.

| 4 | **Rg1** | **Bg5!** |

Black must stop 5 Rc1, even at the cost of a Bishop.

| 5 | **Rxg5+** | **d5+** |

A clever interposition.

| 6 | **Rxd5+** | **Ka4** |

On 6 . . . Kb6, 7 Rb5+ Kxc7 (or 7 . . . Ka7 8 Ra5+ and 9 Ra1) 8 Rc5+ and 9 Kd4 wins for White.

continued

Now it seems that White cannot stop the Pawn from Queening. Can't stop the Pawn? No matter!

7	Nb5!	c1 = Q +
8	Nc3 +	Ka3
9	Ra5 +	Kb2
10	Ra2 mate!	

ENDING *14*

Birnov, 1952

White to play and win

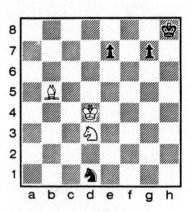

The Knight is chased way up the board and out of play, so that White can execute a pretty mate with Knight and Bishop.

1	Ba4	e5 +

This will enable Black's Knight to escape—temporarily.

2	Nxe5	Nf2

Of course 2 . . . Nb2 fails; 3 Bb3 and 4 Kc3 win the Knight.

3	Ke3	Nh3

The alternative 3 . . . Nh1 is hopeless after the reply 4 Kf3.

4	Bd7	Ng5
5	Kf4	Nh7
6	Ng6 +	Kg8
7	Be6 mate	

ENDING **15**

Birnov, 1954

White to play and draw

White creates a drawing device as strange as any I've ever seen!

1 Bc1!

"Un sacrificio a prima vista misterioso," says Porrera's book on the ending.

1	...	Nxc1
2	Ne3	

Apparently intent on stopping the Pawn by 3 Nc4 or 3 Nd1.

2	...	b2
3	Nc4!	

But not 3 Nf5 Nc7 4 Nd6 Nd5!, which stops White from checking at e7.

3	...	b1 = Q
4	Nd6!	
	Draw!	

Black, a full Queen ahead, cannot stop White's perpetual check; 5 Ne7+ Kf8 (of course not 5 . . . Kh8 6 Nf7 mate) 6 Ng6+ Kg8 7 Ne7+, and White draws by repeating the position.

Bondarenko, Kuznetsov

White to play and win

A cute little ending that is sure to charm amateur or expert.

The King flees up the board—and then is forced down to meet his fate.

1   Kf6

Threatens 2 fxg5—instant mate.

1   . . .   Bg8

If instead 1 . . . gxf4, 2 g5 + Kh5 3 g4 mate.

2	fxg5 +	Kh7
3	fxg6 +	Kh8
4	g7 +	Kh7
5	g6 +	Kh6
6	g5 +	Kh5
7	g4 mate	

Who says quadrupled Pawns are weak?

Botvinnik, 1925

White to play and win

Botvinnik composed this study early in his career. The idea is based on a game he won from Livtov. The sudden mate must have come as a shock to Black.

1	g4+	Kh4

For this and his next three moves Black has no alternatives.

2	Bh6	Qxh6

Forced, since other moves by the Queen allow 3 Qh2 mate.

3	Qh2+	Kg5
4	Qd2+	Nf4
5	Qd8 mate	

A pretty little combination, almost the equal of Botvinnik's many beautiful combinations brought about in actual play.

ENDING *18*

Botvinnik, 1939

White to play and win

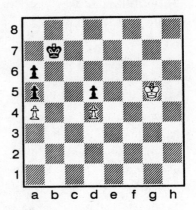

An instructive ending. One would think that all White has to do is win the d-Pawn and it's all over. Let's see.

If 1 Kf6 Kb6! 2 Ke5 Kc7 3 Kxd5 (or 3 Ke6 Kc6) Kd7 4 Kc5 Kc7 5 d5 Kd7 6 Kb6 (or 6 d6 Kd8 7 Kc6 Kc8) Kd6 7 Kxa5 Kxd5 8 Kxa6 Kc6, drawn.

The winning idea is to capture the d-Pawn, but only at a moment when Black cannot take the opposition by moving to d7. The way to do it is to maneuver the King to a8, and remove the Pawns stationed on the a-file, thus:

1	Kf5!	Kb6
2	Kf6!	Kb7
3	Kf7	Kb8

On 3 . . . Kb6, 4 Ke8 is the key move.

4	Ke6	Kc7

Or 4 . . . Kc8 5 Kd6!

5	Ke7	Kc6
6	Kd8	Kd6
7	Kc8	Kc6
8	Kb8	Kb6
9	Ka8	

White wins.

Once the a-Pawns have gone, Black is helpless, since his King cannot get to a6 to maintain the opposition.

Bron, 1926

White to play and draw

A witty miniature in Bron's usual clever style.

> **1 f7**

This seems simple and strong—push on to the Queening square!

> **1 ...**   **Nc7**

Prevents any further advance. Now if 2 Kc4 e1 = Q 3 f8 = Q Qc3 mate.

> **2 Nf2**

Ready to meet 2 . . . e1 = Q with 3 Nd3 + .

> **2 ...**   **Kc2**
> **3 Nd3**   **Kxd3**
> **4 Kd6**   **e1 = Q**
> **5 f8 = Q**   **Qb4 +**
> **6 Ke5**   **Qd4 +**

Or 6 . . . Qxf8, stalemate.

> **7 Kf5**   **Qf2 +**
> **8 Ke5**   **Qxf8**
>   **Stalemate.**

ENDING *20*

Bron, 1958

White to play and draw

Would you expect a stalemate from this weird position?

Watch Bron's master hand manipulate the pieces to the proper squares!

1	Bf7 +	Kh8
2	Bxa2	Be2 +

With the noble object of promoting the Pawn.

3	Kc2	Bd3 +

Of course not 3 . . . f1 = Q 4 Bxc3 + followed by mate.

4	Kb3	Bc4 +

Here if 4 . . . f1 = Q 5 Bxc3 + Kg8 6 Kb4 + Kf8 7 Rf7 + Qxf7 Kxf7 9 Bd4, and a drawn result.

5	Ka4	Bxa2

If 5 . . . f1 = Q, there is an ingenious draw by 6 Bxc3 + Kg8 7 Rg7 + Kf8 8 Bxc4!! Qxc4 + 9 Bb4 + Ke8 (if 9 . . . Kxg7, White is stalemated) 10 Re7 + Kd8 11 Rd7 + Kc8 12 Rd8 + Kc7 13 Rd7 + and White forces the draw by perpetual check.

6	Bxc3 +	Kg8
7	Rg7 +	Kf8
8	Rg6	Ng4

If 8 . . . f1 = Q, 9 Rf6 + draws.

9	Rxg4	f1 = Q
10	Rf4 +	Qxf4 +
11	Bb4 +	K moves
	Stalemate.	

ENDING *21*

Bron, 1972

White to play and win

Bron demonstrates the power of a double check, against which even the gods cannot prevail.

1	c7	Rc8
2	Bxh8	Rxh8
3	Ne4	

Threatens 4 Nxd6 followed by 4 c8 = Q.

3	. . .	Kb6

Better than 3 . . . Rc8 4 Nxd6 Rxc7 5 Nb5 + and the Rook goes.

4	Rxh6	Rc8
5	Nxd6	Rxc7
6	Nc8 mate	

ENDING 22

Canal, 1936

White to play and win

White demonstrates the power of a Queen, who so often needs no help to bring about checkmate.

1 Kf5!

The attractive 1 a7 fails in its object, for after 1 . . . c2 2 a8 = Q c1 = Q + 3 Kf5 Qg5 + !, and Black has the better of it.

| 1 . . . | Kxh5 |

This time on 1 . . . c2 there follows 2 Nf4 c1 = Q 3 g3 + Kxg3 + 4 Ne2 + Kf2 5 Nxc1 g3 6 a7 g2 7 a8 = Q g1 = Q 8 Qa2 + Kf3 (forced) 9 Qe2 + Kg3 10 Qg4 + and wins.

2	a7	c2
3	a8 = Q	c1 = Q
4	Qh8 +	Qh6
5	Qe8 +	Kh4
6	Qe1 +	Kh5 or g3
7	Qh1 mate	

ENDING 23

Chekhover, 1937

White to play and win

A unique King wandering is the theme of this beautiful composition.

White's pieces in the lower right-hand corner must stay where they are. So must Black's—if the Bishop moves, Qxg2 mate follows.

It devolves upon White's King therefore to subdue Black's active Knight. He may not move to a White square, since check by the Bishop followed by Queening the f-Pawn would follow. However, moving on black squares only will not permit the King to approach the Knight.

The key: The King must move on black squares only until he reaches a White square, which allows him to lose a move, but a White square that does not permit the Bishop to check.

1	Kb2	Nf7
2	Kc3	Nh8
3	Kd4	Ng6
4	Kc5	Nh8
5	Kb6	

On 5 Kd6 instead, 5 . . . Ng6 follows, and the King may not approach the Knight.

continued

5	. . .	Ng6
6	Ka7	Nh8
7	Ka8!!	

The magic square, which enables the King to lose a move.

7	. . .	Ng6
8	Kb8	Nh8
9	Kc7	Nf7!
10	Kb6	Nh8
11	Kc5	Ng6
12	Kd4	Nh8
13	Ke5	Nf7 +
14	Kf6	Nh8
15	Kg7	Nf7
16	h8 = Q!	

Of course not the hasty 16 Kxf7 when 16 . . . Bc4 + turns the tables.

16	. . .	Nxh8
17	Kxh8	B moves
18	Qxg2 mate	

ENDING *24*

Chekhover, 1948

White to play and draw

The idea of a draw seems hopeless in the face of two passed Pawns, but an ingenious first move initiates the proper procedure.

1 Kg8!

Startling, as one would expect the King to advance instead of retreating. If instead 1 Kg6 h4 2 Rh7 Kg2, and the position of White's King prevents him from checking at g7.

1	...	h4
2	Rh7	h3
3	Rxh3	Kg2
4	Rh7!	f1 = Q
5	Rg7+	Kh3
6	Rh7+	Kg4
7	Rg7+	Kh5
8	Rh7+	Kg6
9	Rg7+	Kh5
	Drawn.	

Chlubna, 1968

White to play and win

This is one of those delightful compositions where a Knight and Bishop (the Rook is sacrificed on the first move) overcome two Rooks, two Knights, a Bishop, and three Pawns (to say nothing of the King, who is checkmated).

1	Rh8+	Kxh8
2	Nxe8+	Kg8
3	Nf6+	Kh8

Of course 3 . . . Kf8 allows 4 Bd6 mate.

4	Ng4+	Kg8
5	Nh6+	Kf8
6	Bd6+	Ke8
7	Ng8	Rdc8

The King needs a flight square.

8	Nf6+	Kd8
9	Kf7	

Closing in.

9	. . .	Ra7
10	Ne8	Rcc7
11	Be7+	Kc8
12	Nd6 mate	

Cohn, 1928

White to play and draw

One must know when to capture the Queen and when not to do so!

1   Kf2

Obviously 1 Rxe4+ Kxe4 2 Kf2 Kd6 3 Ke1 Kc2 loses easily.

1	. . .	b4
2	Ke2	

Once again 2 Rxe4+ Kxe4 loses after 3 Ke2 Kd4 4 Kd2 b3! 5 Kd1 (or 5 Kc1 Kc3) Kd3! 6 Kc1 Kc3 and wins.

2	. . .	b3
3	Kd1	

The finesse that saves the game.

3	. . .	Qxe3
	Stalemate.	

Cortlever

White to play and win

This ending combines two themes of which I am fond, a King wandering, and mate by a Pawn. Reason enough to recommend this composition.

1 Qf6

With the brutal threat of 2 Qc6 + and mate next.

| 1 | ... | **Rg6** |
| 2 | **Qc6 +** | **Rxc6** |

Forced, since 2 ... Ka7 3 b6 + cxb6 4 cxb6 + Ka6 5 b7 + is decisive.

| 3 | **dxc6 +** | **Ka7** |
| 4 | **Ke6** | **h5** |

Hoping White will chase the Pawn, when this would follow: 5 Kf5 h4 6 Kg4 h3 7 Kxh3, and Black gets a draw by stalemate.

5 Kd5!

Disregards the passed Pawn and the possibility that it will turn into a Queen.

5	...	**h4**
6	**Kc4**	**h3**
7	**Kb4**	**h2**
8	**Ka5**	**h1 = Q**
9	**b6 +**	**cxb6**
10	**cxb6 mate**	

Dorogov, 1969, First Prize

White to play and win

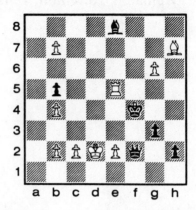

A remarkable ending! After a great deal of feverish scurrying by the Queens, White decides the issue by two little Pawn moves!

1	Re4 +	Kxe4

Better than 1 . . . Kg5 2 g7.

2	g7 +	Kd4
3	c3 +	

But not 3 g8 = Q, when 3 . . . Qe3 + 4 Ke1 h1 = Q is mate.

3	. . .	Kc4
4	Bg8 +	Bf7
5	b8 = Q	

Threatens 6 Qc7 + Kd5 7 Bxf7 + Ke4 8 Bg6 + Kd5 9 g8 = Q + and mate next move.

5	. . .	h1 = Q
6	Bxf7 +	Qxf7
7	Qc7 +	Qxc7
8	g8 = Q +	Qd5 +
9	Kc2!	Qxg8
10	e4!	

Black's two Queens are helpless to prevent mate by an insignificant Pawn.

10	. . .	any
11	b3 mate	

Drumaren, Lowenton, 1962

White to play and win

A bit old-fashioned in concept, this still makes a pleasing study.

1	d8 = Q +	Nxd8
2	Qa3 +	Ke8
3	Bxf8	

Threatens 4 Qe7 mate.

3	...	Rxf8
4	Bd7 +	Bxd7
5	Nd5	

Threatens mate in two ways.

5	...	Qxe5

Guards against both—but only for the moment!

6	Qe7 +	Qxe7
7	Nxc7! **mate**	

The smothered mate is always attractive.

Duizov, 1966

White to play and win

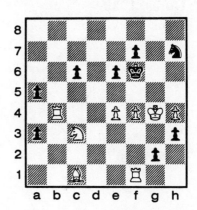

With both Rooks attacked, and with Black threatening to Queen a Pawn, White relies (justifiably) on the amazing power of double check to smite the enemy hip and thigh.

1	Rg1	h2

On 1 . . . axb4 2 Kxh3 bxc3 3 Bxa3 leaves an easy win.

2	Rb1	hxg1 = Q
3	Bb2	

The Bishop is en prise, but then so is Black's Queen.

3	. . .	Qxb1
4	Nd5 +	Kg6
5	Ne7 +	Kh6
6	Ng8 +	Kg6
7	h5 mate	

Duras, 1939

White to play and win

Known primarily for his strength as a player, Duras managed to construct a number of fine endings. In this one, Black's pieces fight vainly to keep the Rook from getting to the King, but each time one door shuts, another one opens.

| 1 | f7 | Bxf7 |

Forced, to prevent 2 f8 = Q+.

| 2 | Rg4 | Bb3 |

Stops 3 Ra4 mate.

| 3 | Rg1 | |

Threatens 4 Rxa1+ and mate next.

| 3 | ... | Nc2 |
| 4 | Rg5 | |

Now aims at 5 Ra5 mate.

| 4 | ... | d5 |
| 5 | Kb6 | d4 |

Covers the square g8.

| 6 | Kc7 | |

To which there is no defense.

White wins.

Evreinov, 1959, First Prize

White to play and win

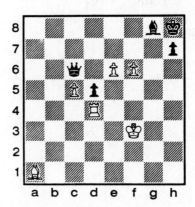

A magnificent combination; the surprise moves in this ending remind one of a blazing Alekhine brilliancy.

White's chief weapon is the Bishop modestly placed at a1, and the threat of discovered check. But how does White start the machinery going?

1	Re4	dxe4 +
2	Kg2	e3 +
3	Kg1	Bf7
4	exf7	Qxc5
5	f8 = Q + !	Qxf8
6	f7 +	Qg7 +
7	Kh2	
	White wins.	

Evreinov, 1962

White to play and win

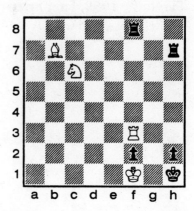

Some pretty play forces the win.

    1   Rf7!

A startling first move! The natural 1 Rxf8 fails after 1 . . . Rxb7 2 Nd4 Rb1 + 3 Kxf2 Rf1 + 4 Kxf1 stalemate.

    1 . . .   Rhxf7

Quick loss follows 1 . . . Rfxf7: i.e. 2 Ne7 + Rf3 3 Bxf3 mate.

2	**Ne7 +**	**Rf3**
3	**Nc8!**	**R8f5**
4	**Be4**	**Rf6**
5	**Nd6**	**R6f4**
6	**Bxf3 +**	**Rxf3**
7	**Ne4**	

White wins.

The Knight will inflict mate next move.

Evreinov, 1966

White to play and win

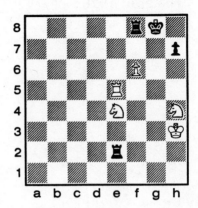

White spurns a Rook that is offered, but this material inferiority is compensated for by his superior position. This turns out to be decisive.

1   Nf5!

Involves a beautiful winning idea: 2 Ng5 Rxe5 3 Nh6+ Kh8 4 Ngf7+ Rxf7 5 Nxf7+ Kg8 6 Nxe5 and wins.

1 ...	**Rxe4**
2 Nh6 +	

Better than the immediate capture 2 Rxe4, when 2 ... Rxf6 draws easily.

2 ...	**Kh8**
3 Rg5	

Threat: 4 Rg8+ Rxg8 5 Nf7 mate.

3 ...	**Re3 +**
4 Kh4	**Re4 +**
5 Kh5	**Re5**
6 Rxe5	**Rxf6**
7 Re8 +	**Kg7**
8 Rg8 mate	

ENDING 35

Filaterov, 1926

White to play and win

Like a good thriller, the issue is in doubt until the very last moment.

1	b7	Rb2
2	Nb5!	

Now if 2 . . . Rxb5, 3 Rxd5 pins the Rook and wins.

2	...	Nh4

Intending 3 . . . Nf3 followed by 4 . . . Rxh2 mate.

3	Rd1	Nf3
4	Ra1 +	Kb4
5	Rb1	Rxb1 +
6	Kg2	Rg1 +
7	Kxf3	Rg8
8	Na7	

Threatens 9 Nc8, blocking the Rook.

8	...	Rb8
9	Nc6 +	

White wins.

Fritz, 1939

White to play and draw

Fritz demonstrates that a piece may be irretrievably lost, but not the game.

A neat rendering in miniature of an old Troitzky theme.

| 1 | Bg7 | Rg6 |

There's nothing in 1 . . . Rf3 after 2 Be6+ in reply.

2	Bxh8	Rh6
3	Bf1 +	Kb4
4	Ba1!	Rh1
5	Kb2	Rxf1

Drawn by stalemate.

Fritz, 1947

White to play and win

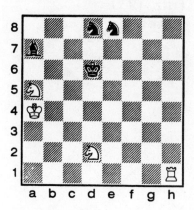

The pieces are spread far and wide, but White manages to create an artistic arrangement of the four Knights in just a few moves.

1	**Rh8**	Kd7

Or 1 . . . Ke7 2 Rh7 + Nf7 3 Nc6 + and the Bishop falls.

Black is playing to trap the Rook.

2	**Rh7 +**	Kc8
3	**Rxa7**	Nc7

Threatens 4 . . . Kb8.

4	**Ndc4**	Kb8
5	**Rb7 +**	Nxb7

A King move allows 6 Nb6 mate.

6	**Nc6 +**	Kc8
7	**Nb6 mate**	

A pretty picture.

Fritz, 1950

White to play and win

Wherein the modest little Pawn proves irresistible.

> **1 Ra1**

Threatens mate as well as 2 Rc1 winning a piece.

> **1 ...**   **Bb7**
> **2 Ra7**   **Nb5**

An ingenious defense.

> **3 Rxb7**   **Nd6 +**
> **4 Ke7**   **Nxb7**
> **5 b4**
>   **White wins.**

The King simply walks over to the paralyzed Knight, removes it, and then Queens his Pawn. Simple, like all truly great schemes.

Gentner, 1952

White to play and win

A surprise sacrifice provides a target for White—but strangely enough his aim is directed in a different direction!

1	Kg2	Kg6
2	Kf3	Kf5
3	e4 +!	dxe4 +
4	Kg3!	Kg5
5	e3	Kf5
6	Kh4	Ke5
7	Kg5	Kd5
8	Kf5	Kc5
9	Ke5!	

But not 9 Kxe4 Kc4, and the position is drawn.

9	...	Kb5
10	Kd5!	Kb4
11	Kd4	Kb5
12	Kc3	Ka4
13	Kc4	

White wins.

Giningev, 1930

White to play and draw

Wherein the Bishop zooms down the length of the board to
bury himself, and save the life of the King.

| 1 | h7 | Bb1 |

Otherwise the Pawn will become a Queen.

| 2 | d3 | Nxe2 |

If 2 . . . Nxd3 + 3 exd3 Bxd3 4 Be5 Bxh7 5 Bxg3, and the position
is drawn.

| 3 | Ba1! | Nxd3 + |
| 4 | Ka3 | Bc5 + |

Forces the King to a white square where the Knight at d3 can
check him, and meanwhile clear the way for 6 . . . Bxh7.

| 5 | Kb3! | |

But not 5 Ka4 Nb2 + 6 Bxb2 Bxh7 and Black wins.

5	. . .	N3c1 +
6	Kb2!	Bxh7
	Stalemate.	

An artistic finish.

ENDING *41*

Gogberashvili, 1973

White to play and win

After ten forcing moves that leave Black no choice, White sacrifices a Knight to finish with a pretty Pawn mate.

1	Ng7	Kh6
2	g4	Kh7

If 2 . . . Rh7 or 2 . . . Bh7, then 3 g5 mate.

3	Nh5	Kh6
4	Nf4	Kh7

Again if 4 . . . Rh7 or 4 . . . Bh7, then 5 g5 is mate.

5	Nxh3	Kh6
6	Nf4	Kh7
7	h3!	Kh6
8	h4	Kh7
9	h5	Kh6
10	g5 +	Kh7
11	Ng6!	hxg6
12	hxg6 mate	

Gorgiev, 1929

White to play and win

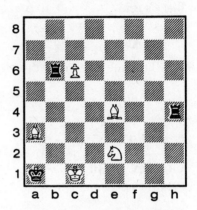

Gorgiev composes a beautiful variation on the famous Saavedra theme, distinguished by three sacrifices of pieces.

1	c7	Rc6 + !

On 1 . . . Rh8 instead, White plays 2 Bc5, followed by 3 Bd4 +, and removes the Rook.

A pretty try is 1 . . . Rxe4 2 c8 = Q Rc6 + 3 Qxc6 Rc4 + 4 Nc3! Rxc6 5 Bb2 mate.

2	Bxc6	Rc4 +
3	Kd2	Rxc6
4	Bd6!	Rxd6 +
5	Nd4!	

One brilliant move follows another!

5	. . .	Rxd4 +
6	Kc3	Rd1

Threatening 7 . . . Rc1 +.

7	Kc2	Rd4
8	c8 = R	

continued

On 8 c8 = Q instead, 8 . . . Rc4 + 9 Qxc4 is stalemate. But now Black's reply is forced, to prevent mate on the a-file:

8	. . .	Ra4
9	Kb3!	

Attacking the Rook, and threatening mate; too much for Black.

E N D I N G 43

Gorgiev, 1930
White to play and win

Gorgiev needs little material to create a witty interplay of pieces in this much-admired ending.

Capturing Rook or Bishop leads to a simple draw. So White plays

    1   Rb3 +

. . . which, being check, takes precedence over every other move, and threatens, if the King moves, 2 Bxf6. Black's hand is forced:

1	. . .	Rb6!
2	Rxb6 +	Kc7

After which two of White's pieces are attacked.

    3   Bd8 + !

But not 3 Re6 Kd7, and Black escapes with a draw.

3	...	Kxd8
4	Rb8+	Ke7
5	Kg6!	

White wins by the power of zugzwang—Black is compelled to move, but every move loses!

ENDING 44

Gorgiev, 1936

White to play and draw

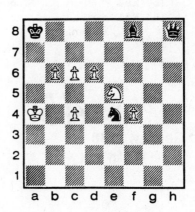

Some startling moves punctuate this fine production!

1	b7+	Ka7
2	b8=Q+	Kxb8
3	c7+	Kb7
4	c8=Q+	Kxc8
5	d7+	Kc7
6	d8=Q+	Kxd8
7	Nf7+	Ke7
8	Nxh8	Kf6

The smoke of battle has cleared; White has won the Queen, but his Knight is in mortal danger. Can he still save the Knight, and the game?

continued

9	f5	Kxf5
10	Nf7	Ke6
11	Nd8 +	Kd7
12	Nb7	Kc7

"The villain still pursued her."

13	Na5	Kb6
14	c5 +!	

Avoids 14 Nb3, when the reply 14 . . . Nc3 is mate.

14	. . .	Nxc5 +

Other moves allow the Knight to escape by way of b3.

15	Kb4	Nb7 +
16	Ka4	Nxa5
	Stalemate.	

E N D I N G 45

Gorgiev, 1938
White to play and win

White attacks and maintains the pressure until mate is forced.

1 Rh1

Threatens nothing less than 2 Nf3—mate on the move.

1	. . .	Rh3
2	Bd7	Rh5
3	Ng4!	

Again with a powerful threat: if 3 . . . Rxh1 then 4 Bf5 is mate.

3	. . .	Rf8 +
4	Kxf8	Rxh1

Black avoids disaster, though White still has the attack.

5	Bf5 +	Kh8
6	Ne5	

New threat of mate by 7 Nf7.

6	. . .	Rh7

Ready to reply to 7 Nf7 + with 7 . . . Rxf7 + 8 Kxf7, stalemate.

7	Ng6 mate

E N D I N G 46

Gorgiev, 1956
White to play and win

His King is cornered, but Black still manages to put up a fight.

1	Rg7 +	Kh8
2	g6	

continued

Now White's idea is to bring his King to f7, and on a Rook check to interpose his Knight at f6.

| 2 | . . . | Nb6 + |
| 3 | Ke7 | |

But not 3 Ke6 Nd5 4 Kxd5 Rd1+ 5 Ke6 Re1+ 6 Kd7 Rxe8, and White's winning chances are gone.

| 3 | . . . | Re1 + |

If instead 3 . . . Nd5 +, then 4 Kf8 Rf1 + 5 Rf7 Rxf7 +, and White wins with 6 Kxf7.

| 4 | Kf7 | |

But not 4 Kf8 Rxe8 + .

4	. . .	Rf1 +
5	Nf6	Rxf6 +
6	Kxf6	Nd5 +
7	Kf7	Nf6

Now if 8 Kf8, Nd7 + is the reply, but . . .

| 8 | Rh7 + | Nxh7 |
| 9 | g7 mate | |

Gorgiev, 1968

White to play and win

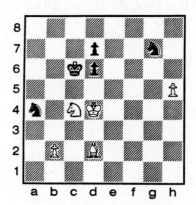

Delightful maneuvering by the minor pieces characterizes this fascinating ending. The final coup is a bit unexpected.

1	h6	Nf5 +
2	Kd3	Nxh6
3	Bxh6	

Black is content to give up his Knight for the advanced Pawn, as he seems to have a draw in sight.

3	. . .	d5

But it's White's turn to move, and as Bronstein once said, "The most powerful weapon in chess is to have the next move!"

4	Ne5 +	Kd6
5	Bf4	Nxb2 +
6	Kc3	Na4 +

On 6 . . . Nd1 + , 7 Kd2 forces the Knight to b2 or f2, where White can win it by 8 Nd3 + .

7	Kb4	Nb6

Safety at last?

8	Nc4 + +	Kc6
9	Na5 mate	

Gorgiev, Rudenko, 1957

White to play and win

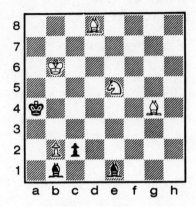

White's two Bishops display frightening power in their pursuit of the enemy King.

1 Bg5

The Pawn must be stopped from advancing.

1	...	Bf2 +
2	Ka6	Bd4
3	Nd3	c1 = Q!
4	Nxc1	Bxb2

Ordinarily, two minor pieces can draw against three, but the terrible Bishops are ready to bear down on the King.

5	Bd7 +	Kb4
6	Be7 +	Kc4
7	Be6 +	Kc3
8	Bf6 +	Kc2

He tries to protect his Bishop,

9	Bb3 +	Kxc1

. . . but it's at the cost of his life.

10 Bg5 mate

A pretty finish!

Gorgiev, Rudenko, 1960

White to play and win

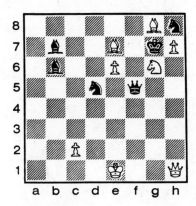

Even more brilliant than White's Queen sacrifice (which leads to mate) is the march of his King along the black diagonal to h4, back to e1, and once again to h4. A startling conception.

| 1 | Bf8+ | Qxf8 |

The alternative 1 . . . Kf6 2 Qh4+ Qg5 3 Qxg5+ Kxg5 4 Nxh8 leads to a prosaic win.

| 2 | Nxf8 | Ba5+ |
| 3 | Kf2 | |

The King must not move to a White square, as a Knight check will uncover an attack on his Queen.

3	. . .	Bb6+
4	Kg3	Bc7+
5	Kh4	Bd8+
6	e7!!	

White needs the square e6, as we shall see.

6	. . .	Bxe7+
7	Kg3	Bd6+
8	Kf2	Bc5+

continued

9	Ke1	Bb4 +
10	c3!!	Bxc3 +
11	Kf2	Bd4 +
12	Kg3	Be5 +
13	Kh4!	Bf6 +
14	Kg4!	Ne3 +
15	Kh5	Bxh1
16	Ne6 mate	

ENDING *50*

Grigoriev, 1923

White to play and win

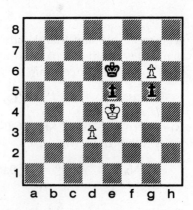

Subtle timing of moves is a characteristic of Grigoriev's pawn endings. This is one of my favorites.

1	g7	Kf7
2	Kf5!	

On the obvious 2 Kxe5 Kxg7 3 Kf5 Kf7 4 Kxg5 Ke6 draws.

2	...	Kg8

Here if Black plays 2 . . . Kxg7 then 3 Kxg5 wins for White.

3	Kg4!	

On 3 Kxg5 e4! 4 dxe4 Kxg7 and draws, but not 3 . . . Kxg7 4 Kf5 e4 5 Kxe4 and White wins.

| 3 ... | Kf7 |

If 3 ... Kh7 4 Kxg5 e4 5 Kf6 and White wins. Or 3 ... Kxg7 4 Kxg5 and White wins.

| 4 Kxg5 | e4 |
| 5 Kh6 | |

But not 5 dxe4 Kxg7 and Black escapes.

| 5 ... | Kg8 |

On 5 ... exd3 6 Kh7, and 7 g8 = Q + is lethal.

| 6 dxe4 | |

White wins.

ENDING 51

Grigoriev, 1928
White to play and win

If there is an undisputed master of King-and-Pawn endings, it is Grigoriev.

He manages to find unusual ideas in the most mundane positions.

| 1 Kd4! | b5 |

continued

The natural continuation. Defending instead against White's Pawn leads to 1 . . . Kb5 2 Kd5! Ka6 3 f4! Kb7 4 f5 Kc7 6 Ke6! Kd8 7 Kf7 b5 8 Kg7 and White wins.

2	f4	b4
3	f5	b3
4	Kc3!	

This is the important move, for 4 f6 leads only to a draw.

4	. . .	Ka3
5	f6	b2
6	f7	b1 = Q
7	f8 = Q +	Ka2

Or 7 . . . Ka5, when 8 Qa8 + wins the Queen.

8	Qa8 mate!

ENDING 52

Grigoriev, 1937
White to play and win

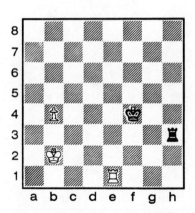

Grigoriev's artistry extends beyond Pawn endings, of which he is an acknowledged master. In this innocent-looking Rook ending, he springs a surprise checkmate.

1 Kc2!

The obvious 1 Ka2 fails after 1 . . . Rd3 2 b5 Rd5 3 Rb1 Ke5 4 Ka3 (or 4 b6 Ra5+) 4 . . . Kd6 5 b6 Kc6 6 b7 Ra5+ and draws.

1	...	Kf5
2	b5	Kf6
3	b6	Rh8
4	Kc3	Rb8
5	Rb1	Ke7
6	Kc4	Kd7
7	Kb5	Kc8
8	Rc1+!	

But not 8 Kc6 Rb7 9 Ra1 Rc7+!

8	...	Kb7
9	Rc7+	Ka8
10	Ra7 mate	

ENDING **53**

Grigoriev, 1937
White to play and win

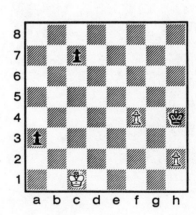

Despite a hidden Black resource, White finds an ingenious way to win.

1	h3	c5
2	Kb1	c4
3	Ka2	

continued

This looks decisive, but Black has a little trick up his sleeve.

3	. . .	c3!
4	Kb3!	

But not the tempting 4 Kxa3 when Black draws by the famous Réti idea: 4 . . . Kg3! 5 f5 Kf4 6 f6 Ke3 7 f7 c2 8 f8 = Q c1 = Q + and draws.

4	. . .	a2
5	Kxa2	

White makes sure that the c-Pawn does not Queen with check.

5	. . .	Kg3
6	f5	Kf4
7	f6	Ke3
8	f7	c2
9	f8 = Q	c1 = Q
10	Qh6 +	

Black's Queen is lost.

White wins.

Grigoriev, 1946
White to play and win

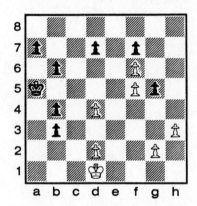

White's problem is that he has to stave off possible mate by the flock of Black's Queenside Pawns coming down the board.

The effort to create a passed Pawn on the Kingside would be refuted thus: 1 g3 Ka4 2 Kc1 (forced) Ka3 3 Kb1 b2 4 h4 Kb3 5 h5 a5 6 h6 a4 7 h7 a3 8 h8=Q a2 mate.

Therefore:

1	Kc1	Ka4
2	Kb2	b5
3	g3	a5
4	h4	gxh4
5	gxh4	d5!

Trying for stalemate, of course.

6	Kb1	Ka3
7	h5	b2
8	h6	a4
9	h7	b3!

With the same noble object.

10	h8=N!	b4
11	Ng6!	fxg6
12	f7	gxf5
13	f8=N!	f4
14	Ne6	f3
15	Nc7	f2
16	Nb5! mate	

ENDING 55

Gulayev, 1956

White to play and win

In this fascinating miniature, White manages to entangle the Rook (in two lines of play). A shrewd Bishop sacrifice serves to advance the career of the Pawns.

1	Be3 +	Kd5
2	h7	Rh4

Or 2 . . . Ra8 3 Bh6! Ke6 4 Bxg7 Kf5 5 Bf8! Rxf8 6 g7 wins.

3	Bg5!	Rh1 +
4	Kg2	Rh5
5	Bf6!	Ke6

Of course not 5 . . . gxf6, 6 g7 wins.

6	Bxg7	Kf5
7	Bh6!	

The key move!

7	. . .	Rxh6
8	g7	

White wins.

ENDING 56

Gurgenidze, 1972

White to play and draw

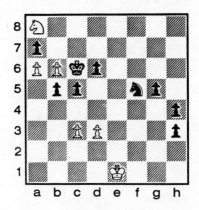

An absolutely delightful ending, with White's Knights alternating in an attack on the King, who is cornered on an edge of the board.

1	b7	h2
2	Kf2	h1 = Q

Delay is dangerous: if 2 . . . h3, 3 b8 = Q h1 = Q 4 Qb7 mate.

3	b8 = N +	Kd5
4	Nc7 +	Ke5
5	Nd7 +	Kf4
6	Ne6 +	Kg4
7	Nf6 +	Kh3
8	Nxg5 +	Kh2
9	Ng4 mate	

Noble work by the Knights!

Gurvich, 1927

White to play and win

In this weird position White evolves an unusual smothered mate.

1	Na6!	Ra7!

If he tries 1 . . . Re7, then 2 Ng6 R7xe8 3 Rxe8 Rxe8 4 Nc7 + and White wins the remaining Rook.

2	Bxc6 + !	Rxc6
3	Nd7 +	Kb7
4	Rb8 +	Kxa6
5	Rb6 +	Rxb6
6	Nxc5 mate	

Gurvich, 1927

White to play and win

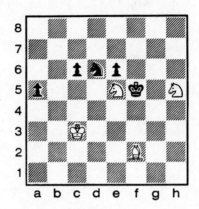

A delightful Knight galloping sets the King up for the kill.

1 Kb3

Moving the threatened Knight away would allow 1 . . . Ne4 + , winning the more valuable Bishop.

1	. . .	Kxe5
2	Bg3 +	Kd5

In this, and the following moves, the King must stay close to the Knight.

3	Nf6 +	Kc5
4	Nd7 +	Kd5
5	Nb6 +	Kc5
6	Na4 +	Kd5
7	Nc3 +	Kc5
8	Bf2 mate	

An elegant finish.

ENDING 59

Gurvich, 1955

White to play and win

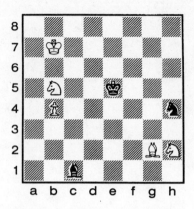

Just as Black's King is about to save the game by capturing the Bishop, the Knights gallop over and ruin his plans.

1	Bh1	Bd2

Goes after the most dangerous unit.

2	Na7	Bxb4

Otherwise 3 b5 follows.

3	Nc6 +	Kf4

Black hopes to capture one of the pieces in the corner.

4	Nxb4	Kg3
5	Nf1 +	Kf2
6	Nd2	Ng2

If Black can get rid of the Bishop (who has no way of escape), his troubles will be over.

7	Nd3 +	Kg1
8	Nf3 +	Kxh1

Wins the Bishop, but at great cost.

9	Nf2 mate	

Gurvich, 1959

White to play and win

Lowly Pawn indeed! This one justifies its existence.

1	Kf2	Nh3 +
2	Kg2	Ng5
3	Be3	

Threatens to win the pinned Knight by 4 Nf7 + .

| 3 | ... | Be7 |

Better than 3 . . . Kh5 4 Bxg5 Kxg5 5 Ne6 + and White wins the Bishop.

4	Nf7 +	Kh5
5	Bxg5	Bxg5
6	Kh3!	

A quiet, waiting move.

| 6 | ... | B moves |
| 7 | g4 mate | |

Gurvich, 1960

White to play and draw

This might be called "drawing by perpetual threat of mate."

1	Ra3 +	Ba7
2	Rxf3	Nd6 + +

On 2 . . . Ne7 + + instead, the reply 3 Kd8 Bg4 4 Rf4 wins a piece.

3	Kc7	Nb5 +
4	Kxc6!	

Costs a Rook, but White has a little plan to offset the loss.

4	. . .	Nd4 +
5	Kc7!	Nxf3
6	Bg8!	

The point! White threatens mate on the move.

6	. . .	Bb8 +
7	Kb6!	Ba7 +
8	Kc7	

Black can no longer afford to try winning.

>   **Drawn.**

Hadac, Machal, 1967

White to play and win

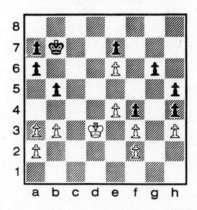

It is unusual to see both Kings trapped by the opposing Pawns. White (the good guy) comes off the victor in the double zugzwang.

1 e5

Makes way for the King to centralize for the attack—and for the defense.

1 . . .   g5

Black naturally tries for the breakthrough by 2 . . . g4.

2	Ke4	g4
3	fxg4	hxg4
4	hxg4	h3
5	Kf3	Kc6
6	g5	Kd5
7	g6	Kxe6
8	b4	

Neither King may move, so White turns to the Queenside.

| 8 | . . . | a5 |
| 9 | a4 | bxa4 |

If 9 . . . axb4, 10 axb5 wins at once.

| 10 | bxa5 | a3 |
| 11 | a6 | |

White wins.

Black's King must eventually move, and allow the g-Pawn to advance and become a Queen.

ENDING 63

Herbstman, 1928

White to play and draw

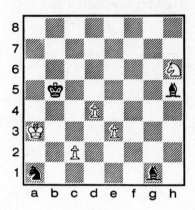

White squeezes out of a tight situation just when everything seems hopeless.

    1 Kb2   **Bxe3**

Unable to save his Knight, Black in turn attacks a Knight, and also threatens 2 . . . Bxd4 + .

    2 Nf5

Protects the Pawn, and in turn attacks the Bishop.

2 ...	Nxc2
3 Kxc2	Bg6
4 Kd3	Bg1
5 Ke4	Bh2

This seems conclusive, as 6 d5 is met by 6 . . . Bd6 and White is out of moves.

    6 Kd5!

He abandons the Knight to its fate.

    6 ...   **Bxf5**
          Stalemate.

Herbstman, 1936

White to play and draw

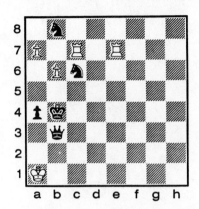

In which the Queen is lured into a cul-de-sac.

   1 Re4+   **Ka3**

With mating threats.

   2 Rxa4+   **Qxa4**

Naturally 2 . . . Kxa4 is inferior on account of 3 a8=Q+ in reply.

   3 a8=Q   **Qxa8**
   4 Ra7+   **Nxa7**
   5 b7!

How embarrassing!

   5 ...   **Qxb7**
           Stalemate.

Herbstman, 1939

White to play and draw

There are some lovely Rook and Queen sacrifices in this innocent-looking position.

1	c7	Rf4 +

The instinctive 1 . . . Rc4 is met by 2 Rxa4, and the threat of
mate is decisive.

2	Kg6	Rc4
3	Rxa4!	Rg4 +!

A desperate move, but what else is there?

4	Rxg4	c1 = Q
5	c8 = Q +!	Qxc8
6	Kf7	Qd8!
7	Rg6	Kh7
8	Rh6 +	Kxh6
	Stalemate.	

ENDING 66

Herbstman, 1953

White to play and draw

Black's Pawn cannot be stopped from Queening, but ingenious play lets White escape with a draw.

	1	Rb5+		Ke6

Moving to the fifth rank by, say, 1 . . . Ke4 is met by 2 Rxb4+ followed by 3 Ra4, and Black can win the Rook, but not the game.

	2	Ra5	Ba3
	3	Bg7	a1 = Q
	4	Re5+	Kf7
	5	Rf5+	Ke6
	6	Re5+	Kd6
	7	Rd5+!	Kc6

If 7 . . . Kxd5, 8 c4+ wins the Queen.

	8	Rc5+	Kb6

Now if 8 . . . Kxc5, 9 cxb4+ wins the Queen.

	9	Rb5+	Ka6

Or 9 . . . Kxb5, 10 c4+.

	10	Ra5+	

Finally, if 10 . . . Kxa5, 11 cxb4+ is the reply. The perpetual check lets White off the hook.

Drawn.

Herbstman, 1961

White to play and draw

The fight centers on Black's Pawn. Winning it would assure White of a draw.

1	Rd7+	Kb8!

Naturally 1 . . . Bxd7, leaving White stalemated, is unthinkable.

2	Rd8+!	Rc8
3	Rd4	Kb7!

Clever defense. If 4 Rxh4, Ra8+ 5 Kb4 Ra4+ wins the Rook and the game.

4	Rb4+	Kc7
5	Rc4+	Bc6

Clearly, if 5 . . . Kb7, 6 Rb4+, and White is content to repeat moves.

6	Rxh4	Ra8+
7	Kb4	Ra4+

This wins the Rook, but not the game.

8	Kc5	Rxh4
	Stalemate.	

Herbstman, Nadareishvili, 1968, First Prize

White to play and draw

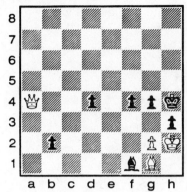

White's material advantage is offset by Black's threats: 1 . . . g3+, and mate next move, and 1 . . . b1 = Q. It needs clever play for White to escape with a draw.

	1	Bxd4	g3+
	2	Kg1	

Of course not 2 Kh1 Bxg2+ 3 Kg1 b1 = Q+ and mates.

	2	. . .	h2+
	3	Kh1	Bxg2+
	4	Kxg2	f3+
	5	Kh1	b1 = Q+
	6	Bg1+	Qb4

Best, as 6 . . . Kh5 7 Qg4+ Kh3 8 Qg5+ Kh7 9 Qg7+ Kxg7 draws by stalemate.

	7	Qxb4+	Kh3

(Black is actually threatening mate!)

	8	Bxh2	f2

And once again!

	9	Qh4+!	Kxh4
	10	Bxg3+	Kxg3
		Stalemate!	

Hevacker, 1936

White to play and win

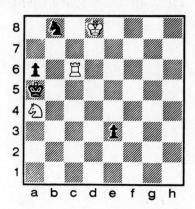

White's pieces are under attack, and he has to head off a dangerous passed pawn. In spite of this, he forces Black's King up the board and into checkmate.

The plausible 1 Re6 fails after 1 . . . Kxa4 2 Kc7 Kb4 3 Kxb8 a 5 4 Kb7 a4 5 Kb6 Kc3 6 Rxe3+ Kb2, and Black manages to draw.

1	Rc4	e2
2	Nb2!	e1 = Q

Or 2 . . . Nc6+ 3 Kc7 e1 = Q 4 Rc5+ Kb4 5 Nd3+ protects the Rook and wins the Queen.

3	Rc5+	Kb6

Here too 3 . . . Kb4 yields to 4 Nd3+.

4	Na4+	Kb7
5	Rc7+	Ka8
6	Nb6 mate	

Holst, 1903

White to play and win

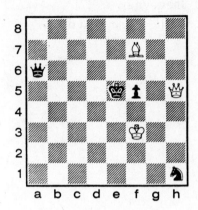

The Queen whirls around the board to achieve her objective—winning the enemy Queen.

1	Qh8 +		Qf6!

Certainly not 1 . . . Kd6 when 2 Qf6+ wins the Queen.

2	Qb8 +		Qd6

But not 2 . . . Kd4 when 3 Qb2+ wins the Queen by x-ray attack.

3	Qb2 +	Qd4
4	Qh2 +	f4 (or 4 . . . Ng3)
5	Qh8 +	

White wins.

Black's King must step aside, and his Queen falls.

Isenegger, 1927

White to play and draw

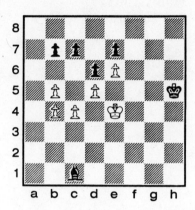

Though outnumbered in material, White gives up four of his five Pawns to achieve a satisfactory result.

1   b6!

Begins an attempt to break through.

1   . . .   cxb6

Forced, since 1 . . . c6 2 dxc6 bxc6 3 b7 wins for White.

2   c5!

Threatens 3 cxd6 exd6 4 e7.

2   . . .   bxc5

Again forced, as after 2 . . . dxc5 3 d6 is decisive.

3   bxc5

Renews the threat of 4 cxd6.

3 . . .	Ba3
4 c6	bxc6
5 dxc6	d5 +
6 Kf5!	

Clearly 6 Kxd5 Bd6 is fatal for White.

6 . . .	Bd6
7 c7	Bxc7
	Stalemate!

Isenegger, 1940

White to play and win

A lovely Bishop move prepares the combination that sends Black's King on a long journey whence he never returns.

1 b7

Otherwise 1 . . . Bc8 ends any winning chances White might have.

1 . . .   **d2**

A powerful defense. Now if 2 b8 = Q + , Kxa1 draws easily, since White cannot win the d-Pawn with check, and a quiet move lets Black Queen his Pawn.

2 Bh8!

Beautiful, and the only way to win.

2 . . .	**d1 = Q**
3 b8 = Q +	

The rest, as we shall see, goes on wheels.

3 . . .	**Kc2**
4 Qb2 +	**Kd3**
5 Qc3 +	**Ke4**
6 Qe3 +	**Kf5**
7 Qe5 +	**Kg6**
8 Qf6 +	**Kh7**
9 Qg7 mate	

ENDING 73

Isenegger, 1950

White to play and win

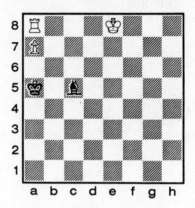

How does White hope to advance his Pawn without abandoning it? For that matter, how does White protect it against the combined attack of King and Bishop?

1	Kd7	Ka6
2	Kc6	Ba3

The only safe move. If for example 2 . . . Ka5 3 Re8 Bxa7 4 Ra8 and wins.

How does White proceed now? If 3 Kc7 Bc5 is the reply, while 3 Kd5 is met by 3 . . . Kb7.

3	Rb8!	Kxa7
4	Rb1!	Bf8

The only safe square for the harassed Bishop!

5	Rh1!

White wins.

The Bishop is trapped! If 5 . . . Bg7 (or 5 . . . Be7), 6 Rh7 wins; if 5 . . . Bb4 6 Ra1 + Kb8 7 Rb1 wins. Finally, if the King moves to a8 or b8, 6 Rh8 pins and wins the Bishop.

Isenegger, 1959

White to play and win

That there is a checkmate is far from obvious. Isenegger pulls a few strings and the pieces jump magically to his bidding.

1	Bd7 +	Kg5
2	Rxh4!	

Brilliant and surprising.

2	...	Kxh4
3	g3 +	Kg5
4	Kg7!	

With a dire threat—mate by 5 f4.

4	...	h4

The only possible defense.

5	f4 +	Kh5
6	g4 mate	

Isenegger, 1964

White to play and win

Simple endings are not always simple. In this one, the first move is decisive.

1   Ke2!!

The threat (after 1 . . . g5) is 2 Kf3. Therefore Black must move his King, but not to the g-file, which would block his Pawn.

1   . . .   Kh2

The point is that this move is forced. Now White can Queen his Pawn with check! The continuation:

2	b4	g5
3	b5	g4
4	b6	g3
5	b7	g2
6	b8 = Q +	Kh1

If instead 6 . . . Kh3, 7 Kf2 wins the Pawn, or if 6 . . . Kg1, 7 Qg3 Kh1 8 Kf2 and mate next move.

7	Qh8 +	Kg1
8	Kf3	Kf1
9	Qa1 mate	

Ivanov, 1966

White to play and win

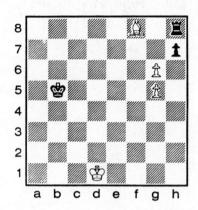

A subtle waiting move assures White of a neat win.

1	g7	Rg8
2	Ke2	Kc6
3	Kf3	Kd7
4	Kg4	Ke8
5	Kh5	Rxf8
6	Kh6!	

Very pretty! Nothing comes of 6 gxf8 = Q + Kxf8 7 Kh6 Kg8, and Black draws the ending.

6	...	Rg8
7	Kxh7	Kf7
8	g6 +	

After which the King must abandon the Rook.

White wins.

Joita, 1954, First Prize

White to play and win

Though Black constructs what seems to be a bombproof position, White proceeds to immobilize the King, and then win the Bishop by the means demonstrated by Loyd in his famous three-move problem "The Love Chase."

1	g6	Be5
2	a6	Bd4

It is clear that the Bishop cannot hold back both Pawns. One of them must become a Queen.

3	g7	Bxg7
4	a7	Bd4
5	a8 = Q	Bf2
6	Qa3	Kc2

Less promising is 6 . . . Ke2, when 7 Qc3 Kd1 8 Qb2 Ke1 9 Qc2 Kf1 10 Qd1 + Be1 11 Qd3 + Kf2 12 Qf3 is mate.

7	Qf3	Kb2
8	Qd3	Kc1
9	Qe2	Kb1
10	Qd2	Ka1
11	Qc2	

Both Kings are in stalemate positions!

White wins by domination. The proof:

If 11 . . . Be1 (or . . . Bg1) 12 Qc1+.
If 11 . . . Be3 12 Qc3+.
If 11 . . . Bd4 12 Qd1+.
If 11 . . . Bb6 12 Qa4+ Kb7 13 Qb4+.
If 11 . . . Ba7 12 Qa4+.

E N D I N G **78**

Jonsson, 1964
White to play and win

Working with only the skimpiest of materials, White fashions a clever win. He keeps Black on the run by a series of checks, and forces the King into the clutches of a Knight fork which costs Black his Queen.

1 Na5!

There is nothing in 1 Nc5 b2 2 c7 b1=Q 3 c8=Q+ Ka7 4 Qa6+ Kb8 5 Nd7+ Kc7, and the position is drawn.

1	. . .	b2
2	c7	b1=Q
3	c8=Q+	Qb8

continued

The alternative 3 . . . Ka7 loses to 4 Nc6 + Kb6 5 Qb8 + and the Queen falls.

4	Qa6 +	Qa7
5	Qc6 +	Kb8
6	Qe8 +	Kc7
7	Qe7 +	Kb6
8	Nc4 +	Ka6
9	Qa3 +	Kb7
10	Nd6 +	Ka8

On 10 . . . Kb8, 11 Qb3 + forces the King to move to a8.

11	Qf3 +	Kb8
12	Qf8 +	Kc7
13	Nb5 +	

White wins.

E N D I N G **79**

Kabiev, 1973

White to play and win

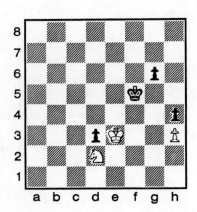

White offers a lesson in accurate timing.

1	Nc4	g5

Threatens 2 . . . g4 and a quick draw.

2	Kf3	Ke6

There is no solace in 2 . . . g4+ 3 hxg4+ Kg5 4 Nd2 h3 5 Kg3 and White wins.

3	Kg4	Kf6
4	Nd2	Kg6
5	Ne4	Kh6
6	Kf5	Kh5
7	Nf6+	Kh6
8	Ng4+	Kh5

The King is now held fast, and helpless to prevent mate. So White can disregard the passed Pawn.

9	Kf6	d2
10	Kg7	d1 = Q
11	Nf6 mate	

ENDING 80

Kalandatze, 1957
White to play and draw

Drastic action is required, since Black threatens 1 . . . Qe2+ 2 Kxg3 Qg2+ 3 Kh4 Qg4mate. There is also a dangerous-looking Pawn on h3 to be disposed of.

1	Ra5+	Qxa5
2	Ra1+	Kb2

continued

On 2 . . . Kb4 instead, 3 Rxa5 Kxa5 4 Kxg3 is easy for White.

| | 3 | Rxa5 | h2 |

Now what?

4	Rb5 +	Kc2
5	Rc5 +	Kd2
6	Rd5 +	Ke1
7	Re5 +	Kf1

Black is happy; the checks have ceased.

8	Kxg3	h1 = Q
9	Re1 + !	Kxe1
	Stalemate.	

ENDING 81

Kalandatze, 1966

White to play and win

White weaves a mating net around the enemy King. Every piece in his little army takes part in the encirclement.

| 1 | Rd8 + | Kg7 |
| 2 | h6 + | Kf6 |

Now what? If 3 Bg5 + Ke5 4 Bf4 + Kxe4, and the King slips out.

3	Rd6 + !	Qxd6
4	Bg5 +	Ke5
5	Bf4 +	Kf6
6	e5 + !	

Of course not the hasty 6 Bxd6, when Black is stalemated.

6	. . .	Qxe5
7	Bg5 mate	

A nice finish.

ENDING 82

Kalandatze, 1967

White to play and win

Trapped in a corner, the Rook must be lost; but a neat mate is the best revenge.

1	Rg4	Nh3

Obviously, if 1 . . . Nf3 2 Rf4 + wins the Knight.

2	Nd7 +	Kf7
3	Ne5 +	

The Knight is now strongly placed for an attack on the King.

3	. . .	Kf8
4	Rh4	Ng5

continued

Here if 4 . . . Nf2 + , 5 Ke2 is fatal.

| 5 | Rxh8 | Nh7 |

Confines the Rook, and threatens to win it by 6 . . . Kg7.

6	Nd4	Kg7
7	Nf5 +	Kxh8
8	Ng6 mate!	

ENDING 83

Kalandatze, 1970
White to play and win

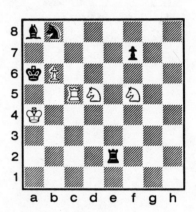

White's little combination ties Black up completely, and the two Knights speedily dispatch the King.

| 1 | Ra5 + | Kb7 |
| 2 | Ra7 + | Kc8 |

On 2 . . . Kc6 instead, 3 Nd4 + is uncomfortable for Black.

3	Rxa8	Ra2 +
4	Kb5	Rxa8
5	b7 +	Kxb7
6	Nd6 +	Ka7

Alas, there is no choice!

| 7 | Ne7 | |

Threatens 8 N7e8 mate.

7	. . .	Nd7

Meets the threat, but opens up another—just as fatal!

8 Nc6 mate

ENDING **84**

Kalandatze, Tavariani, 1967
White to play and win

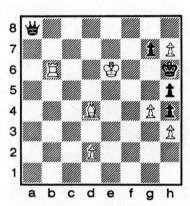

To win this, White must inveigle Black's King and Queen into a cul-de-sac.

1 h8 = Q +

This leaves Black no choice.

1	. . .	Qxh8
2	Kf5 +	Kh7

This too is forced, as after the interposition 2 . . . g6 +, the capture 3 Rxg6 + wins the Queen.

3	Rh6 +	Kxh6
4	g5 +	Kh7
5	g6 +	Kg8

continued

Clearly 5 . . . Kh6, 6 Be3 mate would not do.

6	Bc5	Qh6
7	Be3	Qh8
8	Ke6	Kf8
9	Kd7	Qg8

With a view to escape, as 9 . . . Kg8 10 Ke7 is hopeless.

10   Bc5 mate

ENDING *85*

Kaplan, 1966
White to play and win

The winning move is a Knight fork, that useful tool of the combination player.

1	h7	c2
2	Bb2	

A pretty move, but Black has resources too.

2	. . .	c1 = Q
3	Bxc1	Bh8
4	Nf4	Kf5
5	Bb2	Be4

Aiming indirectly at the Pawn.

6	Bxh8	Kg4
7	Nd5	Bxh7
8	Nf6+	

Wins the Bishop and the game.

ENDING 86

Kashdan, 1959

White to play and win

White must Queen all three of his Pawns before he can subdue his opponent.

1	Kxg3	Kd4!

Follows the Réti maneuver: Black is ready to aid his Pawn by 2. . .Ke3, and also prepared to stop White's advanced Pawn by 2. . .Ke5.

2	h6	Ke3
3	h7	f2
4	h8 = Q	f1 = Q
5	Qe5+	Kd2!
6	Qf4+	Qxf4+
7	Kxf4	b5
8	h5	b4

continued

9	h6	b3
10	h7	b2
11	h8 = Q	b1 = Q
12	Qd4 +	Ke2!

As good as any; Black cannot avoid an exchange of Queens.

13	Qe4 +	Qxe4 +
14	Kxe4	b5
15	h4	

Black's Pawn is more advanced than his opponent's, but now he must lose a move or two with his King to insure it against loss. If, for example, 15. . .b4 16 Kd4, and the Pawn is not long for this world.

15	. . .	Kd2
16	Kd4	Kc2
17	Kc5	Kc3!!

Again the beautiful Réti idea. If 18 K × b5 Kd4, and Black catches the Pawn.

18	h5	b4
19	h6	b3
20	h7	b2
21	h8 = Q +	
	White wins.	

The rest is a book win.

Kasparyan, 1934

White to play and win

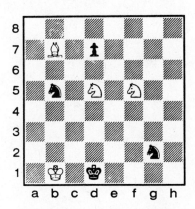

There are various forms of mate involving all four Knights. This one is quite attractive.

| 1 | Ba6 | Na3 + |

The alternative is 1. . .Na7, when there follows 2 Bf1 Ne1 3 Nc3 + Kd2 4 Ne4 + Kd1 5 Ne3 mate.

2	Kb2	Nc2
3	Bf1	Nge1
4	Nc3 +	Kd2
5	N34 +	Kd1
6	Nfg3	

Threatens mate by the Bishop.

6	. . .	Nd4
7	Be2 + !	Nxe2
8	Nf2 +	Kd2
9	Nf1 mate	

ENDING **88**

Kasparyan, 1936

White to play and win

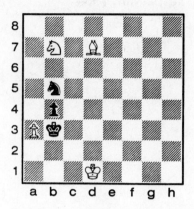

A brilliant miniature in which the Knights' dancing around is reminiscent of Vandercrotele's masterpiece, as well as of Capablanca's celebrated maneuver in his game against Yates at New York in 1924.

The plausible 1 Bxb5 allows 1. . .bxa3 and Black escapes with a draw, while 1 Nc5+ Kc4 is no better.

	1	a4!	Nc3+

Obviously the dangerous Pawn must be removed, but not by 1. . .Kxa4 2 Nd6 Ka3 3 Nxb5+ Ka2 4 Be6+ b3 5 Nd4 and White wins.

2	Kc1	Nxa4
3	Na5+	

The white Knight wheels around like an eagle, aiming to set up the King for the kill, while the Bishop forces him to defend his own Knight.

3	. . .	Ka3
4	Nc4+	Kb3
5	Nd2+	Ka3
6	Nb1+	Kb3
7	Be6 mate	

A lovely finish.

Kasparyan, 1955

White to play and win

A pleasing miniature, wherein Kasparyan creates an artistic effect by what problem composers describe as a "model mate," in the middle of the board. The moves are clear-cut and need no commentary.

1	Bf5	Kd4
2	Ne6 +	Ke5
3	Bh3	Bc2
4	d4 +	Kd5
5	Kb5	Bh7
6	Kb4	Bg8
7	Kc3	Bxe6
8	Bg2 mate	

ENDING 90

Kasparyan, 1958

White to play and win

An attractive little two-Bishop mate—at close quarters.

1	Re8+	Kb7
2	Re7+	Ka8
3	Kc6	

Closing in for the kill.

3	...	Qb8!

On 3. . .Qf2 instead, White continues 4 Bb6 Qc2+ 5 Bc5 Qa4+ 6 b5, and there is no defense.

4 Re8

But not the seductive 4 Bxf3 Qb7+ 5 Rxb7, and Black is stalemated.

4	...	Qxe8
5	Bxe8	f2
6	Kc7	f1=Q
7	Bc6+	Ka7
8	Bb6+	Ka6
9	b5+	Qxb5
10	Bb7 mate	

ENDING 91

Kasparyan, 1962

White to play and win

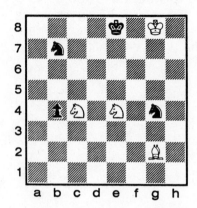

White drives the opposing Knights from pillar to post, and then concludes with a combination that effects checkmate by a picturesque arrangement of Knights.

1	Bh3	Nh6 +

The alternative is 1 . . . Nh2, when there would follow 2 Bc8 Nd8 3 Nf6 + Ke7 4 Nd5 + Ke8 5 Nd6 mate.

2	Kg7	Nf7
3	Bc8	Nbd8
4	Nf6 +	Ke7
5	Nd5 +	Ke8
6	Ncb6	

Threatens 7 Bd7 mate, and forces the reply.

6	. . .	Ne5
7	Bd7 +	

White is not to be denied.

7	. . .	Nxd7
8	Nc7 +	Ke7
9	Nc8 mate	

Beautiful!

Kastnelson, 1966

White to play and draw

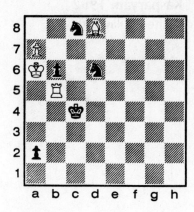

White begins with a surprise move and ends with a surprise move.

    1   Ra5

Attacks the a-Pawn and forces the reply.

1	**...**	**bxa5**
2	**a8 = Q**	**a1 = Q**
3	**Qc6 +**	**Kb4**

Black holds on to the important Pawn without which he could not win.

4	**Qc3 +**	**Kxc3**

Clearly, if 4 . . . Qxc3 5 Bxa5 + regains the Queen and draws.

5	**Bxa5 +**	**K moves**
	Stalemate.	

ENDING 93

Kastnelson, 1971

White to play and win

A pleasurable ending, but practical as well, since it illustrates an idea that comes up often in actual play.

1	g4	Kg2

If 1 . . . hxg3 2 hxg3, and the Pawn cannot be overtaken.

2	g5	Kxh2
3	g6	h3
4	g7	Kh1

On 4 . . . Kg1 instead, the continuation would be 5 g8 = Q + Kf2 6 Qf7 + Kg2 7 Qg6 + Kf2 8 Qf5 + Kg2 9 Qg4 + Kh2 10 Kd6, and White wins the Pawn.

5	Kd6!	h2
6	Ke5	Kg1
7	g8 = Q +	Kf2

The alternative is 7 . . . Kh1 8 Qa2 Kg1 9 Kf4 h1 = Q 10 Kg3 and White wins.

8	Qa2 +	Kg1
9	Kf4	h1 = Q
10	Kg3	

White wins.

Mate is forced.

Kastnelson, 1972

White to play and win

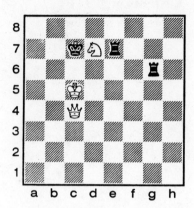

A surprise sacrifice, letting Black take a piece with check, leads to an elegant mate.

    1 Ne5!   Rxe5 +

Refusing the offer by 1 . . . Rg5 lets White win slowly but surely by 2 Kb4 + .

    2 Kd4 +   Rc6

Forced, as after 2 . . . Kd6 3 Qa6 + wins a Rook.

    3 Qf7 +   Kd6
    4 Qf6 +   Re6
    5 Qd8 mate

A pretty form of epaulet mate.

Kazantsev, 1953

White to play and win

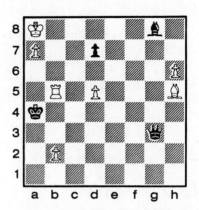

A beautiful smothered mate by a Pawn! Roycroft says, "The composer worked for fifteen years on this theme before this wonderful version was produced." (Another revision of this idea appears in *The Fireside Book of Chess,* by Chernev and Reinfeld.)

1   Rb7

Threatens 2 Bd1 + Ka5 3 b4 + Ka6 4 Be2 + and mate next move.

1	. . .	Qe5
2	Bd1 +	Ka5
3	b4 +	Ka6
4	Be2 + !	

He goes there anyway!

4	. . .	Qxe2
5	Kb8	Qe5 +
6	Kc8	Qe8 +
7	Kc7	Bxd5

No better is 7 . . . Qe5 + 8 d6 Qxd6 + (if 8 . . . Qc3 + 9 Kb8 wins) 9 Kxd6 Kxb7 10 b5 Kxa7 11 Kc7 and White wins.

8	a8 = Q + !	Qxa8
9	Rb6 +	Ka7
10	b5	

continued

Threatens 11 Ra6 mate.

10	...	Bb7

Now that his opponent's pieces are all boxed in, White finishes with a flourish.

11	Ra6 +	Bxa6
12	b6 mate	

ENDING 96

Kazantsev, 1964

White to play and win

Kazantsev is at his best in this splendid creation.

1	e7	Qa3 +
2	Rb4	Qa7 +

The dangerous Pawn must be removed.

3	Kxc4	Qxe7
4	Nxg6 + !	fxg6
5	Bf6 + !	Qxf6
6	Kd5 +	Kg5
7	h4 +	Kf5
8	g4 +	hxg4
9	Rf4 + !	Bxf4
10	e4 mate	

Kiselev, 1965

White to play and win

A little combination disposes of Black's Queen. When a new Queen appears, a little combination removes the new Queen.

1	Nf6+	Kf7

Quick loss follows 1 . . . Kh8 2 Rh2 Qb8 3 Rh3 Qc8 4 Rh5 and the coming discovered check will be decisive.

2	Nd5+	Kg8

Obviously 2 . . . Ke8 or 2 . . . Ke6 allows a Knight fork, winning the Queen.

3	Ne7+	Kh8
4	Ng6+	Kg8
5	Rf8+	Qxf8
6	Nxf8	d3

Clearly Black has no time for 6 . . . Kxf8.

7	a7	d2
8	a8=Q	d1=Q
9	Nd7+	Kf7
10	Qf8+	Ke6
11	Nxc5+	Ke5

Moving to the d-file allows 12 Qd8+, winning the Queen.

12	Qe7+	Kf4

continued

Better (for the moment) than 12 . . . Kf5, when 13 Qg5 is checkmate.

| 13 | Qg5+ | Kf3 |
| 14 | Qh5+ | |

Skewers Black's Queen.

White wins.

ENDING 98

Klinkov, 1967

White to play and win

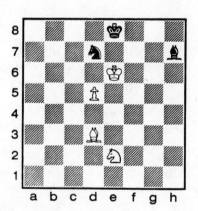

A miniature that charms us with its simple, crystal-clear solution. A study that deserves to be called classic.

1	Bb5	Bg8+
2	Kd6	Kd8
3	Bxd7	Bxd5

Trusting that this will draw, since two minor pieces cannot win against one minor piece.

4 Nd4!

Forms a nice little column with this beautiful winning move.

| 4 . . . | B any |

White wins.

White's Knight mates at e6 or c6, depending on Black's move.

Kofman, 1937

White to play and win

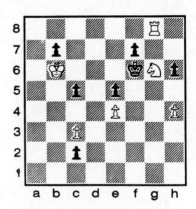

There may be a technical term for the way Black is mated, but I would describe it as a "double epaulet" mate. Black is hemmed in by his own Pawns and a faithless Queen.

1   Ne7

Threatens to stop the Pawn by 2 Rg1.

1	. . .	c1 = Q
2	Nd5 +	Ke6
3	Kc7!	

Threat: mate on the move.

3	. . .	f5
4	Rf8!	

Threat: mate on the move.

4	. . .	fxe4
5	c4!	

Threat: mate on the move.

5	. . .	Qxc4
6	Rf6 +	Kxd5
7	Rd6 mate	

Kopac, 1965

White to play and win

Yes, two Knights can mate—given the opportunity.

1 Nf5+   **Ke6**

If 1 . . . Ke8, 2 Nd6+ costs Black his Rook, while 1 . . . Kf8 allows 2 Rh8 mate, costing him his King.

2 Nd4+   **Ke7**
3 Nc6+   **Ke8**

Now 3 . . . Ke6 allows 4 Nd8+, while 3 . . . Kf8 falls into instant mate.

4 Rh8+   **Rf8**

Or 4 . . . Kd7 5 Nce5+ Nxe5 6 Nxe5+, and White snaps off the Rook next move.

5 Kg7

Threat: 6 Rxf8 mate.

5 . . .   **Rxh8**
6 Nf6 mate!

A pretty finish.

Kopac, Sindelev, 1972

White to play and win

The Bishop just about reaches safety, but in doing so unfortunately imperils the King.

1	Rg3+	Kxh5
2	Bf7	Bf5
3	Bxg6+	Bxg6
4	Kf6	Be8

The Bishop flees to the only safe square.

5	Rg8	Bd7
6	Rd8	Bg4

For the third time the Bishop has no choice, but now the blow falls.

7	Rh8 mate!	

Kopaiev, 1967

White to play and win

Black seems to be holding his own in an ending that looks easy, but is helpless against a move that combines an attack on his Rook with a threat of mate.

1	d7	Rd4
2	Ke7	g2
3	Rg5	Re4 +
4	Kd6	Rd4 +
5	Kc6	Rc4 +
6	Kd5	Rc2
7	d8 = Q	Rd2 +
8	Kc6	Rxd8
9	Kc7	

White wins.

Korolkov, 1950
White to play and draw

Refined endgame play is required until the very last move!

    1 e6!

The attractive 1 d6 loses after 1 . . . d2 2 d7 d1 = Q 3 Kc7 Qa4 4 d8 = Q Qxa5 + 5 Kd7 Qxd8 + (brutal, but efficient) 6 Kxd8 Kd5 7 Ke7 Kxe5, and Black wins.

1	. . .	Kd6
2	e7	Kxe7
3	Kc7	d2
4	d6 +	Ke6!
5	d7	d1 = Q
6	d8 = Q	Qxd8 +
7	Kxd8	Kd6
8	Kc8!	

Advancing the Pawn would cost its life.

8	. . .	Kc6
9	Kb8!	Kb5

Now it would seem the Pawn is lost.

    10 Kb7!

Strong, as it forces Black to take the Pawn.

continued

10	...	Kxa5
11	Kc6	

Drawn.

The White King is just in time: 11 . . . h5 12 Kd5 h4 13 Ke4 h3 14 Kf3 h2 15 Kg2, drawing by the skin of his teeth.

ENDING *104*

Korolkov, Dolivkanov, 1939

White to play and win

As unlikely a position as you will ever see! The solution is reminiscent of Steinitz's most beautiful game. It was played at Hastings in 1895 against Bardeleben and was highlighted by five offers of the Rook on the seventh rank.

1	Rh5 +	Qh7
2	Rxh7 +	Kg8

On 2 . . . Kxh7 there follows 3 Bd3 + Kh6 4 Bxf2 and White wins despite the flock of Pawns at Black's disposal.

3	Rxg7 +	Kf8

If 3 . . . Kxg7, 4 Bc3 + and 5 Bxg2 wins for White, or if 3 . . . Kh8, 4 Rh7 + Kg8 5 Rh8 + wins.

4	Rxf7+	Ke8
5	Rxe7+	Kd8
6	Rxd7+	Kc8
7	Rxc7+	Kb8
8	Rxb7+	Kc8

Here if 8 . . . Ka8, 9 Bxg2 fxe1 = Q 10 Rb1+ wins for White.

9	Rc7+	Kb8
10	Rc8+	Ka7
11	Ra8+	Kxa8
12	Bxg2+	

White wins.

ENDING *105*

Korolkov, Mitrofanov, First Prize

White to play and draw

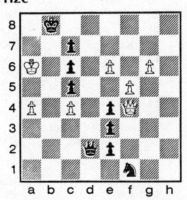

This is one of the most remarkable compositions I have ever come across. Not the least of its attractions is the possibility of sacrificing the Queen by one side or the other. The possibility, revealed in the notes, occurs no less than seven times! Only the word "wonderful" can do justice to this superb creation.

1   Qe5

continued

Threatens 2 Qh8+ followed by mate. If instead 1 g7 (or 1 e7) Qa5+! 2 Kxa5 Kb7 followed by 3 . . . e1 = Q mate, unless White plays 3 Qh4, whereupon Black replies 3 . . . Nd2, and mates with the Knight.

1	. . .	Qa5 + !
2	Kxa5	Kb7
3	Qb2 +	Ka7
4	Qb8 + !	

One good sacrifice deserves another! Note that 4 Qxe2 would have lost by 4 . . . Nd2 and the Knight mates.

4	. . .	Kxb8
5	Ka6	e1 = Q
6	g7!	

Now if 6 . . . Qg3 (to restrain the g-Pawn), 7 e7 wins for White.

6	. . .	Qa5 + !
7	Kxa5	Kb7
8	g8 = Q	e2
9	Qa8 +	Kxa8
10	Ka6	e1 = Q
11	e7	Qa5 + !
12	Kxa5	Kb7
13	e8 = Q	Nd2

Threatens 14 . . . Nb3 mate, as well as 14 . . . Nxc4 mate.

14	Qa8 + !	

Careful with the Queen sacrifice! If instead 14 Qb8 + Kxb8 15 Ka6 Kc8 stops White's passed Pawn, while his own moves on to e1.

14	. . .	Kxa8
15	Ka6	

Of course not 15 f6 Kb7 followed by mate with the Knight.

15	. . .	Nxc4
16	f6!	

Avoids 16 a5, when this would follow: 16 . . . Ne5 17 f6 Nd7 18 f7 Nb8 mate.

16	. . .	Nd6
17	f7	Nxf7
18	a5	

And White will be stalemated next move. Magnificent!

ENDING *106*

Kovalenko, 1966
White to play and win

The heavy pieces do the threatening, but it remains for a humble Pawn to administer the *coup de grâce*. A nice rendition of a pretty theme.

| 1 | Rf5 + | d5 + |

Necessary, since 1 . . . Kb6 allows 2 Rxg8.

2	Rxd5 +	Ka4
3	Rxg8	Rc2 +
4	Kd3	Rd2 +
5	Kc3!	

Sacrifices the Rook! If instead 5 Ke4, Rxb2 draws easily.

| 5 | . . . | Rxd5 |
| 6 | Kc4 | |

continued

Attacks the Rook, and also threatens mate.

| 6 | ... | Ra5 |
| 7 | Rg3 | |

New threat of mate.

7	...	Bf8
8	Ra3 +	Bxa3
9	b3 mate	

ENDING **107**

Kralin, Kuznetsov, 1966
White to play and win

Fascinating play occurs when the three Pawns passed on the seventh rank all become Queens!

White may not Queen his Pawn, since after 1 a8 = Q there follows 1 . . . h1 = Q + 2 Kg3 Qh2 + 3 Kf3 Qf2 mate. Therefore:

| 1 | Bf3 | a1 = Q |
| 2 | a8 = Q! | |

Now if 2 . . . Qxa8 3 Re1 + Kf2 4 Bxa8 Kxe1 5 Kg3 and White wins.

2	...	h1 = Q +
3	Bxh1	Qxa8
4	Re1 +	Kh2
5	Be4!	

Of course not 5 Bxa8, stalemate. Meanwhile White threatens mate.

5	...	Qa1

Playing for 6 Rxa1, stalemate.

6	Rb1!	
	White wins.	

ENDING **108**

Kricheli, 1957
White to play and draw

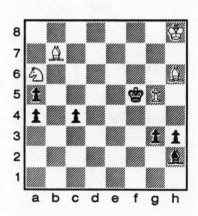

Black has a flock of dangerous-looking Pawns on their way to become Queens. How does White head them off? How does he save the game?

1 Bc8 +

Failure would follow 1 Bg7 g2 2 Bd4 g1 = Q 3 Bxg1 Bxg1 4 Bc8 + Ke4 5 Bxh3 a3, and the Pawn cannot be stopped.

continued

1	. . .	Kg6
2	Bxh3	g2

A nice sacrifice to gain the initiative. If instead 2 . . . Bg1, 3 Bg7 is the effective reply.

3	Bxg2	Be5 +
4	Kg8	a3
5	Be4 +	Kh5
6	Bb1	c3
7	Nc5	c2!

On 7 . . . a2 8 Bxa2 c2 9 Nd3 draws.

8	Bxc2	a2
9	Nb3	a4
10	Na1!	Bxa1
11	Bg6 +!	Kxg6

Of course if 11. . . .Kg4, 12 Bf7 is easy.

12	Bg7!	Bxg7
	Stalemate.	

ENDING 109

Kruchkov, 1938

White to play and draw

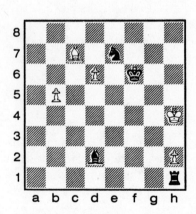

It takes unusual skill to escape with a draw in this position.

    1 d7

White's only threat, of course.

| 1 . . . | Ng6+ |

Black must play to eliminate the dangerous Pawn.

| 2 Kh3 | |

On 2 Kg3 Bf4+ 3 Bxf4 Ke7 wins the Pawn; so also after 2 Kg4 Ne5+ 3 Bxe5+ Ke7.

| 2 . . . | Nf4+ |
| 3 Bxf4 | |

Otherwise 3 . . . Ne6 restrains the Pawn.

| 3 . . . | Ba5 |
| 4 b6! | |

An important link in the combination.

| 4 . . . | Bxb6 |
| 5 Be3+ | |

A tempo that gains an important diagonal.

5 . . .	Bc7
6 d8=Q+	Bxd8
7 Bd4+	Ke7
8 Bc5+	

Forces the King away from the black squares.

| 8 . . . | Ke8 |
| 9 Bg1! | |

The point! The threat is now 10 Kg2, winning the Rook.

| 9 . . . | Rxg1 |
| Stalemate. | |

ENDING *110*

Kubbel, 1916

White to play and draw

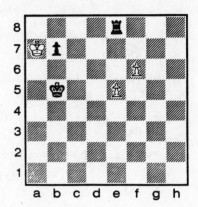

Kubbel's artistry is evident in this little offering where two Pawns outwit a Rook. "A little jewel," says Staudte.

1	f7	Rf8
2	e6	b6

Prevents 3 e7, when 3 . . . Rxf7 pins the remaining Pawn, and wins.

3	Kb7	Kc5

The plan 4 Kc7 Kd5 5 Kd7 Ke5 6 Ke7 fails after 6 . . . Ra8 in reply.

4	e7!	Rxf7
5	Ka6	Rxe7

Forced.

Stalemate.

Kubbel, 1927

White to play and draw

White sacrifices all his worldly goods to escape with a whole skin!

The ambitious 1 f7 is refuted 1 . . . cxd6+ 2 Ke8 Nf6+ 3 Ke7 Nh7, and Black wins. Therefore:

    1 b6!

Threatens 2 dxc7+ and finis.

1	...	Bxb6
2	a5	Bxa5
3	f7	cxd6+
4	c7+	Bxc7+
5	Kd7	Nf6+
6	Kc6	Nh7
7	f8=Q	Nxf8

       Stalemate.

Kubbel, 1931

White to play and win

That Black's King and Queen can be crowded into mate seems hard to believe, but watch Kubbel's fine Italian hand!

1	Qc3+	Kb6
2	Ba7+	Kxa7
3	Qa5+	Kb8
4	Qxb5+	Kc8
5	Qb7+	Kd8
6	Qb8+	Qc8
7	Qb3	

Heading for g8.

7	...	e6
8	Qb7	h3
9	Kf6	h2
10	Qb4	

White wins.

ENDING **113**

Kubbel, 1937

White to play and draw

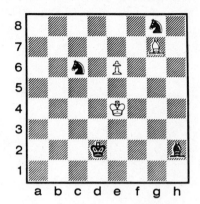

Kubbel illustrates two neat drawing ideas in the short space of four moves!

1 e7!

Sacrifices a lovely Pawn!

1 ... **Ngxe7**

If 1 ... Ncxe7 2 Be5 Bg1 3 Bd4 Bh2 4 Be5 White draws by repeating the position, since if Black exchanges Bishops, he cannot force mate with two Knights.

2 Bh6+! **Ke2**
3 Bf4

The same idea? Not at all!

3 ... **Bg1**
4 Be3 **Bxe3**

        Stalemate.

Kujoth, 1972

White to play and draw

Kujoth has contributed some clever miniature games to the literature of chess. Here he turns his hand to endgame composition with an attractive study.

    1   Rxa7 + !

White must play energetically, since he is threatened with mate at g1 and g2. So he begins with a sacrifice.

    1   . . .   **Nxa7**

If 1 . . . Kb6 2 Qc7 + Kxb5 3 Rxb7 + , and White draws easily.

    2   Nc7 +   **Kb6**
    3   Na8 +   **Qxa8**

White must capture, or submit to perpetual check by 3 . . . Ka6 4 Nc7 + Kb6 5 Na8 + , etc.

    4   Qb8!   **Qxb8**
           Stalemate.

Kuznetsov, 1967

White to play and win

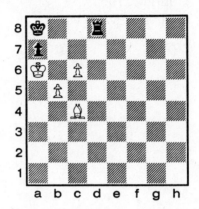

A simple-looking position, but there are subtleties concealed.

1 b6

There is nothing in 1 c7, when 1 . . . Rd6 + 2 Ka5 Kb7 refutes the move.

1 . . .   **Rd6**

But not 1 . . . axb6 2 c7 Rc8 3 Bd5 mate.

2 Bd5!

On 2 Bb5 instead there follows 2. . .Kb8 3 c7 + Kc8 4 Kxa7 Rxb6 5 Kxb6 and Black is stalemated.

2 . . .   **Rxd5**
3 c7   **Ra5 +**
4 Kxa5   **Kb7**

Of course, 4 . . . axb6 + is met by 5 Ka6, and mate next.

5 bxa7   **Kxa7**
6 c8 = R!
               White wins.

Liburkin, 1931

White to play and win

A couple of clever underpromotions do the trick.

1 d8 = N

Of course not 1 d8 = Q, when 1 . . . Nc6+ ends the Queen's short career. The actual move holds Black's King fast. The threat is now 2 f6, Queening the Pawn.

1	. . .	Nxf5
2	Kxa4	Nd6
3	c5	Nb7
4	c6!	Nxd8
5	c7	Nb7

Now if 6 c8 = Q, Black is stalemated.

6	c8 = R	Nxa5
7	Rc5	Nb7

Alas, the only move!

8 Rc6 mate

Liburkin, 1939

White to play and win

Pawns may be the soul of chess, but lovely ideas may often be expressed without them. Liburkin contributes this beauty:

1 Kg1

Releases the Bishop for active duty.

1 . . .   Nf4

No better is 1 . . . Bb3 2 Bxd5 Bxd5 3 Ne3 +, followed by 4 Nxd5, and the three pieces against one is a theoretical win.

2	Ne3 +	Kh3
3	Nxd1	Ne2 +
4	Kf1	Ng3 +
5	Kf2	

White returns the piece, since moving to g1 instead leads to perpetual check and a draw.

5	. . .	Nxh1 + +
6	Kg1	Bf6

Of course not the natural move 6 . . . Ng3, when the reply 7 Nf2 is checkmate.

7 Kxh1   Bd4

continued

White seems to be in trouble now; his king is stalemated, and his other pieces cannot move without loss. But there is a brilliant solution to his dilemma!

8	Nf5!	Bxh8
9	Nf2 mate!	

ENDING 118

Lommer, 1967

White to play and win

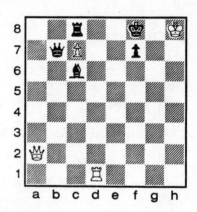

Wherein Black's King is betrayed by his good friends.

1	Qa3 +	Ke8
2	Rd8 +	Rxd8
3	Qf8 +	Kxf8
4	cxd8 = Q +	Be8
5	Qd6 +	Qe7
6	Qh6 mate	

Mann, 1913
White to play and win

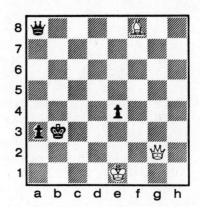

A masterpiece of precise endgame play with Queens on the board. It is fascinating throughout its length.

| 1 | Qg8+ | Ka4 |

Naturally, not to a black square, since a Bishop check would win the Queen by discovered attack.

| 2 | Qc4+ | Ka5 |
| 3 | Bd6 | |

Threatens a decisive Bishop check.

3	...	Kb6
4	Bc7+	Ka7
5	Qc5+	Kb7
6	Qd5+	Ka7
7	Bb6+	Kb8
8	Qd7!	Qa6
9	Qc6	

Threatens the life of the Queen by 10 Bc7+ Ka7 11 Bb8+.

| 9 | ... | Qb7 |
| 10 | Qd6+ | Ka8 |

White decides to remove the passed Pawns, lest they become obstreperous.

continued

11	Qxa3+	Kb8
12	Qd6+	Ka8
13	Qd8+	Qb8
14	Qd5+	Qb7
15	Qa5+	Kb8
16	Qe5+	Ka8
17	Qe8+	Qb8
18	Qxe4+	Qb7
19	Qe8+	Qb8
20	Qa4+	Kb7
21	Qb5!	

To which a King move loses instantly: if 21 . . . Kc8, 22 Qc6+ wins, or if 21 . . . Ka8, 22 Qa6+ wins.

| 21 | . . . | Qg8 |

The best chance; other squares offer the Queen less hope. Black squares are out of the question; e8 is guarded, and the other choices are 21 . . . Qc8 22 Bc5+ Ka8 (on . . . Kc7 23 Qb6+ Kd7 24 Qd6+ and mate at e7) 23 Qa5+ Kb7 24 Qb6+ and mate next; or 21 . . . Qa8 22 Ba5+ Kc8 (22 . . . Ka7 23 Qb6 mate) 23 Qe8+ Kb7 24 Qe4+! Ka6 (or 24 . . . Kc8 25 Qe6+ Kb8—not 25 . . . Kb7 26 Qb6+ and mate next—26 Qd6+ and mate in two) 25 Qc4+! and Black has an unhappy choice of 25 . . . Kxa5 26 Qa2+ winning the Queen, or 25 . . . Kb7 26 Qc7+ and mate in one, or 25 . . . Ka7 26 Qc5+ and mate in two.

| 22 | Bd8+ | Kc8 |

Or 22 . . . Ka8 23 Qc6+ Ka7 (or 23 . . . Kb8 24 Bc7+ forces quick mate) 24 Bb6+ Ka6 25 Bc7+, and mate in two.

| 23 | Qc6+! | Kb8 |

Of course not 23 . . . Kxd8 24 Qa8+, winning the Queen.

| 24 | Bc7+! | Kc8 |

On 24 . . . Ka7, 25 Qb6+ and mate next.

25	Bd6+	Kd8
26	Qc7+	Ke8
27	Qe7 mate	

ENDING *120*

Mitrofanov, 1967, Third Prize
White to play and win

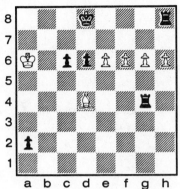

A remarkable ending—a great masterpiece. Roycroft says of it, "Great tension. White declines to capture Black's Queen, and himself offers Black his Bishop four times. A fairy-tale triumph of mind over matter."

1	g7	a1 = Q +

If instead 1 . . . Re8, 2 f7 a1 = Q + 3 Bxa1 Kc7 (threatens instant mate), 4 fxe8 = N + wins. Or if 1 . . . Kc7, 2 Bb6 + forces mate.

2	Kb7!	

If 2 Bxa1 Kc7, "and one of the Rooks mates fiendishly next move," says Roycroft.

2	. . .	Rxg7 +
3	hxg7	

But not 3 fxg7 Qxd4.

3	. . .	Qh1
4	gxh8 = Q +	Qxh8
5	f7	Qh6

The Queen must cover f8 and f6.

6	Be3	Qxe6
7	Bg5 +	

continued

The promising-looking 7 f8 = Q + allows Black an escape by 7 . . . Kd7.

7	. . .	Qe7 +

White may not now play 8 f8 = Q mate, as he is in check.

8	Kxc6

White wins.

8 . . . Qxg5 allows 9 f8 = Q mate. Would you believe that this beauty won only Third Prize in an endgame tourney?

ENDING *121*

Mitrofanov 1967, First Prize
White to play and win

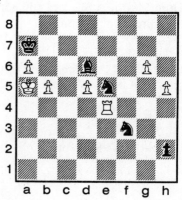

A diamond with a flaw, but a diamond nevertheless!

1	b6 +	Ka8
2	Re1!	Nxe1
3	g7	h1 = Q

A pretty possibility is this: If instead 3 . . . Nc4 + 4 Kb5 h1 = Q 5 g8 = Q + Bb8 6 a7 Na3 + 7 Kc6 Qh2 8 axb8 = Q + Qxb8 9 b7 + Ka7 10 Qg1 + Ka6 11 Qb6 mate.

4	g8 = Q +	Bb8
5	a7	Nc6 +
6	dxc6	Qxh5 +
7	Qg5!	

A beautiful sacrifice to win.

7	. . .	Qxg5 +
8	Ka6	Bxa7
9	c7!	

White wins.

The desperate 9. . .Qa5 + 10 Kxa5 Bxb6 + 11 Kxb6 is *not* stalemate, as Black still has a Knight on the board.

The flaw: One line of the draw runs this way: 2 . . . Nc4 + 3 Kb5 Nxb6 4 Kxb6 Nxe1 5 g7 h1 = Q 6 g8 = Q + Bb8 7 Qg7 Qg1 + ! 8 Qxg1 Ba7 + .

Moravec, 1925

White to play and draw

A tricky little devil! One would expect the King to approach the Pawns, with a view to removing Black's dangerous Pawn, or to save one of his own Pawns from capture. Both moves are will-o'-the-wisps that lead to loss.

Observe these possibilities:

1 Ke5 Kg2 2 h4 Kxf2 3 h5 Kg3 4 h6 f2 5 h7 f1 = Q 6 h8 = Q Qa1 +, and Black wins the Queen.

1 Kf5 Kg2 2 h4 Kxf2 3 h5 Kg3 4 h6 f2 5 h7 f1 = Q + 6 Kg6 Qf8, and Black wins.

The right way:

	1	Kd5!	Kg2

But not 1 . . . Kxh2 2 Ke4 Kg2 3 Ke3, and White wins.

	2	h4	Kxf2
	3	h5	Ke2

Drawn.

Nadareishvili, 1937

White to play and win

Not so complicated, nor as difficult as most of Nadareishvili's creations, this does have a lovely long-distance mate.

1	Bd6	b5
2	Bb4	h1 = Q +
3	Bxh1	Ka2
4	Bd5 +	Kb1
5	Ba3	b4
6	Bb3	bxa3
7	Bg8	a2
8	Bh7 mate	

Nadareishvili, 1948, First Prize

White to play and win

A struggle takes place over the Queening of the Rook Pawn. But just as Black disposes of his most powerful enemy, the blow descends.

1 b5!

There is nothing but a draw after 1 Rc6 a2 2 Rc5 a1 = Q 3 Ra5 + Qxa5 4 bxa5.

1 **...**	**Bxb5**
2 **d6!**	**cxd6**

If instead 2 . . . a2, 3 d7 a1 = Q 4 d8 = Q + Kb7 5 Qd5 + and White wins.

3 **Rxd6**	**a2**
4 **Rd1**	**Bd3**
5 **Ra1**	**Bb1**

Puts the Rook out of business.

6 **Ke7**	**Kb7**
7 **Kd6**	**Kb6**
8 **Ke5**	**Kb5**
9 **Kf4**	**Kb4**
10 **Kg3**	**Kb3**
11 **Kxg2**	**Kb2**
12 **Bh2**	**Kxa1**
13 **Be5 mate!**	

ENDING *125*

Nadareishvili, 1950
White to play and win

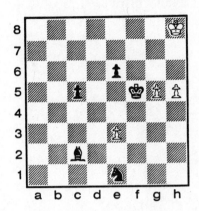

White is outnumbered in material, but he does have two dangerous-looking passed Pawns.

1	g6	Kf6

If instead 1 . . . e5, 2 g7 Bb3 3 h6 Nf3 4 h7 Ng5 5 g8 = Q wins.

2	g7	Bh7!
3	e4	

On 3 Kxh7 Nf3, 4 g8 = Q Ng5 + forces a draw by perpetual check.

3	. . .	Nf3
4	e5 +	Nxe5
5	Kxh7	Nf3
6	g8 = Q	Ng5 +
7	Qxg5 +	Kxg5
8	h6	c4
9	Kg7	c3
10	h7	c2
11	h8 = Q	c1 = Q
12	Qh6 +	

White wins the Queen and the game.

Nadareishvili, 1955

White to play and draw

White escapes by means of an unusual stalemate idea.

    1 Rf2 +

The natural 1 f7 leads to 1 . . . b3 2 f8 = Q h2 3 Rf1 b2 + 4 Kd2 Nc4 + 5 Kc3 h1 = Q 6 Rxh1 Rxh1, and Black wins.

1	. . .	Ka1
2	f7	h2
3	Rxh2	Rxh2
4	f8 = Q	b3
5	Qxa3 +	Ra2
6	d5!	Rxa3

Or 6 . . . b2 + 7 Qxb2 + Rxb2 8 Bd4 a3 9 d6 Ka2 10 d7 Rb8 11 Bf6, and a draw.

7	Bd4 +	Ka2
8	Bb2	
	Stalemate.	

ENDING *127*

Nadareishvili, 1957, First Prize

White to play and win

A lovely ending, quite in keeping with Nadareishvili's subtle, original, and profound style.

    1   Rd7+

Of course not 1 Nc3 (to keep the pawn from Queening), for then 1 . . . Rxe7 2 Bxe7 Kxc3 would follow.

1	. . .	Kc4
2	Rc7+	Kb3
3	Rc3+!	Kxa2
4	Ra3+	Kb1
5	b7	Re8
6	Ra8	Rxa8
7	bxa8=B!	

Naturally, Queening the Pawn allows a draw by stalemate.

7	. . .	Ka2
8	Bd5+	Kb1
9	Ba3	b4
10	Bb3	bxa3
11	Kd2	a2
12	Bc2 mate	

Nadareishvili, 1957
White to play and win

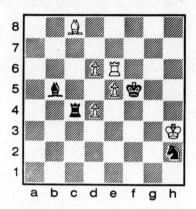

White begins with a discovered check, and then just when Black is about to equalize, finishes with a discovered check and mate.

1	Re8 +	Ke4
2	d7	Bxd7
3	Bxd7	Nf3
4	e6	Ng5 +
5	Kg4	Nxe6
6	Bxe6	Rxd4
7	Bc4 mate	

Nadareishvili, 1958

White to play and win

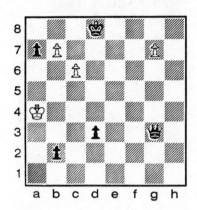

Nadareishvili's fund of original ideas never seems to run dry.

    1   b8 = Q +

The alternative 1 g8 = Q + fails after 1 . . . Qxg8 2 b8 = Q + Ke7 3 Qxg8 b1 = Q and Black equalizes.

1	. . .	Qxb8
2	g8 = Q +	Kc7
3	Qg3 +	Kc8
4	Qg4 +	Kc7
5	Qd7 +	Kb6
6	c7!	Qg8

If 6 . . . Qxc7 7 Qb5 mate. On 6. . .Qf8 7 c8 = Q wins, or if 6 . . . Qb7, 7 c8 = N + Ka6 8 Qd6 + Qb6 9 Nxb6 b1 = Q 10 Nd5 + Kb7 11 Qc7 + Ka8 12 Qc8 + Qb8 13 Nc7 mate.

    7   c8 = N + !

Of course not 7 c8 = Q Qa2 + 8 Kb4 b1 = Q + .

7	. . .	Kc5
8	Qd6 +	Kc4
9	Qb4 +	Kd5
10	Ne7 +	

White wins the Queen and the game.

Nadareishvili, 1961

White to play and win

White has several Rook moves that look good, but only one of them does the trick that forces checkmate.

1   Rg5!

If instead 1 Rxg7 Kh2 2 Kb6 h3 3 Kc5 Kh1 4 Kd4 h2, and Black draws. Or if 1 Rg6 (extremely plausible) Kh2 2 Kb6 h3 3 Kc5 Kh1 4 Kd4 h2 5 Rg3 g5 6 Ke3 g4, and Black will be stalemated. Finally, if 1 Kb6 g5! 2 Kc5 Kh2 3 Ra1 g4 4 Kd4 g3 5 Ke3 g2 6 Kf2 h3 7 Rd1 g1 = Q + 8 Rxg1, stalemate. (A lot of play in a simple-looking position!)

1	. . .	g6
2	Kb6	Kh2
3	Kc5	h3
4	Kd4	Kh1
5	Ke3	h2
6	Rg3	g5
7	Kf2	g4
8	Ra3	g3 +
9	Kxg3	Kg1
10	Ra1 mate	

ENDING *131*

Nadareishvili, 1961

White to play and draw

A clever Queen sacrifice at the last moment saves the game for White.

| 1 | Rd5 | h2 |
| 2 | Rd1 + | Ka2! |

Moving to the b-file instead would allow White to queen his b-Pawn with check.

| 3 | Rh1 | Bg1 |
| 4 | Ka6 | g5 |

If instead 4 . . . d5, 5 b5 d4 6 b6 d3 7 b7 d2 8 b8 = Q d1 = Q 9 Qg8 + Kb2 10 Rxh2 + Bxh2 11 Qxg6, and the position is drawn.

5	b5	g4
6	b6	g3
7	b7	g2
8	b8 = Q	gxh1 = Q
9	Qg8 +	Kb2

If 9 . . . d5 instead, there follows 10 Qxd5 + Qxd5, and White is stalemated.

| 10 | Qd5! | |

Brilliant! Black must play 10 . . . Qxd5, and White gets the draw by stalemate.

ENDING *132*

Nadareishvili, 1962
White to play and win

It's hard to tell who has the advantage, but it takes only five moves to clarify the position.

1   b7

But not 1 Rxb3 + Kxb3 2 b7 Nb6 + 3 Kc7 b1 = Q with a draw.

1	...	b1 = Q
2	Rxb3 +	Qxb3

Or 2 . . . Kxb3 3 b8 = Q + Kc2 4 Qxb1 + Kxb1 5 Kb7 and White wins.

3   bxa8 = R + !

If instead 3 bxa8 = Q + Kb2 4 Qb7 Ka1! 5 Qxb3, and Black gets a draw by stalemate.

3	...	Kb2
4	Rb8	Qxb8 +
5	Kxb8	

White wins.

Nadareishvili, 1965
White to play and win

A trickly little devil, which is bound to trap the unwary solver before he suspects any danger.

1	Ke2	c3
2	g8 = R!	

If instead 2 g8 + ! (certainly natural enough) there follows 2 . . . d1 = Q + 3 Kxd1 c2 + 4 Kd2 (or 4 Kxc2 stalemate) c1 = Q + 5 Kxc1, and the game is drawn by stalemate.

2	. . .	Kb2
3	Rg1	

But not 3 Rc8 Kc2 4 Rd8 Kc1, and Black draws.

3	. . .	Kc2
4	Rf1	Kb3
5	Kd3	Kb2
6	Rg1	Kb3

If 6 . . . d1 = Q + 7 Rxc1 c2 8 Rd2 wins.

| 7 | Rb1 + | |

White wins.

Nadareishvili, 1970

White to play and draw

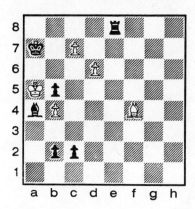

A somewhat complex study, but fascinating nevertheless.

1	d7	c1 = N

On 1 . . . c1 = Q instead 2 dxe8 = Q wins for White. After Black's actual move, he's the one who threatens mate.

2	Bxc1	Bxc1 = N

If instead 2 . . . bxc1 = Q, White does not play 3 dxe8 = Q, since hat allows 3 . . . Qxc7 mate, but continues with 3 c8 = Q Rxc8 4 dxc8 Qxc8 (on other moves by Black's Queen, 5 Qb7 + forces a draw by stalemate), and White is stalemated.

Meanwhile, Black threatens mate on the move.

3	c8 = N +	Kb7
4	Nd6 +	Ka7
5	Nc8 +	

But not 5 Nxb5 + Bxb5 6 Kxb5 Rd8 7 Kc6 Kb8 8 Kd6 Nd3 9 b5 Nc5, and Black wins.

5	. . .	Rxc8
6	dxc8 = N +!	Kb7
7	Nd6 +	Kc6
8	Nxb5	Bxb5
	Stalemate.	

Nadareishvili, 1970

White to play and draw

Pawn endings are deceptive. Under a guise of simplicity, they often conceal subtleties. Herewith a case in point.

1 e4

The proper starting move. If instead 1 d4 h4 2 e4 h3 3 exd5 h2 4 d6 + Kxd6 5 Kb8 h1 = Q, and Black wins.

1	...	d4
2	e5	h4
3	e6	h3
4	e7	h2
5	e8 = R!	

On 5 e8 = Q there follows 5 . . . h1 = Q + 6 Qe4 Qf3 7 Qxf3 (there's nothing else!) gxf3, and Black wins.

5	...	h1 = Q +
6	Re4	Qxe4 +

Or 6 . . . Qc1 7 Re7 + Kd8 8 Rc7!, and White draws.

7	dxe4	h5
8	e5	h4
9	e6	h3
10	e7	h2
11	e8 = N +	Kc8

continued

Black must play to confine White's King.

12 Nd6+ Kc7

Avoiding the perpetual check leads to this: 12 . . . Kd7 13 Kb8 h1 = Q 14 a8 = Q Qxa8+ 15 Kxa8 Kxd6 16 Kb7 Kd5 17 d3, and the position is a draw.

13 Ne8+
Drawn by repetition of position.

ENDING **136**

Neidze, 1958
White to play and draw

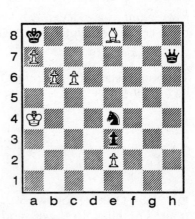

White resolves what might be a troublesome situation with five deft moves.

1 c7

Threatens mate on the move in two different ways.

1 . . . Nc5+
2 Kb5 Qf5

Seems to hold everything. Now if 3 Bc6+ Nb7+ 4 Ka4 (if 4 Ka6 Qa5 is mate) Qc2+ 5 Kb5 Qc5+ wins for Black.

3	c8 = Q +	Qxc8
4	Bc6 +	Nb7
5	Ka6!	Qxc6
	Stalemate.	

ENDING *137*

Neidze, Kalandatze, 1967
White to play and win

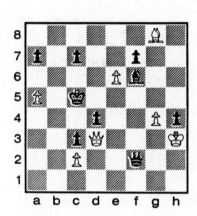

Black's King seems doomed to be mated. In nearly all variations his exit is blocked by Queen and Bishop. For variety there are some discovered checks that win the Queen.

1	exf7	Bh8

The other possibilities are:

1 . . . Bd8 2 f8 = Q + Qxf8 3 Qc4 + Kd6 4 Qd5 + Ke7 5 Qe6 mate.

1 . . . Be7 2 Qc4 + Kd6 3 Qd5 + Kxd5 4 f8 = Q +, and White wins the Queen.

1 . . Bg5 2 f8 = Q + Qxf8 3 Qc4 + Kd6 4 Qb4 +, and White wins the Queen.

1 . . . Bg7 2 Qc4 + Kd6 3 Qd5 + Ke7 4 Qe6 + Kf8 (if 4 . . . Kxe6 5 f8 = Q + and White wins the Queen) 5 Qe8 mate.

continued

2	Qc4 +	Kd6
3	Qd5 +	Ke7
4	Qe6 +	Kf8
5	Qe8 +	Kg7
6	Qe5 +	Kf8
7	Qc5 +	Kg7
8	f8 = Q +	Qxf8
9	Qg5 mate	

E N D I N G *138*

Nestorescu, 1951, First Prize
White to play and win

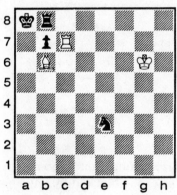

The King must subdue Black's fleet-footed Rook before applying the finishing touches.

1   Rc3

With a powerful threat of mate on the move.

1	...	Rh8
2	Kg7	

Taking the Knight instead wins a piece, but not the game.

2	...	Re8
3	Kf7	Rh8

A pretty defensive attempt is 3 . . . Re7 + 4 Kf8 Kb8 5 Rd3 and mate follows.

4   Bd4

Keeps Black on the run.

4	. . .	Rd8
5	Ra3 +	Kb8
6	Be5 +	Kc8
7	Rc3 +	Kd7
8	Rc7 mate	

A fine creation by the talented Romanian composer.

ENDING *139*

Ol'myutzky, 1960
White to play and draw

This looks like the typical stalemate-in-the-corner theme, but you may be in for a little surprise.

1	Kh7	Kf7

Or 1 . . . a4 2 Kxg6 Kg8 3 h7+ Kh8 4 Kh6 a3 5 g6 a2 6 g7 mate.

2	e4	a4
3	e5	a3
4	e6 +	Kxe6
5	Kxg6	a2
6	h7	a1 = Q
7	h8 = Q	Qxh8
	Stalemate.	

Pasternak, 1969

White to play and win

A charming ending, with two Bishop sacrifices (one of them taken with check), a Queen sacrifice, and for the *coup de grâce* a pretty Pawn mate. All this in five moves!

    1 a7!   **Bxh2**

Clearly, 1 . . . Bxa7 2 Be5 mate would not do at all.

    2 Be8!   **Rxe8 +**

Otherwise White makes a new Queen next move.

    3 Kf7

Threatens mate on the move.

    3 . . .   **Rg8**
    4 a8 = Q

Now there are two threats of mate on the move. The poor Rook cannot be in two places at once!

    4 . . .   **Rxa8**
    5 g7 mate

ENDING **141**

Perkonja, 1966
White to play and draw

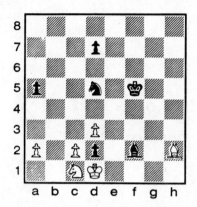

White's method for drawing is ingenious. His Knight, paralyzed by a pin, seems irretrievably lost, but the all-important King is saved by the burial alive of a Bishop, and the heartless abandonment of the Knight.

Something must be done about the Pawn at d2, which is a bone in the throat, but if 1 Kxd2 Be3+ 2 Kd1 Nc3+ wins a piece, while 1 Ne2 Be1 threatening 2 . . . Ne3 mate offers dismal prospects. Therefore:

1	Nb3	a4
2	Nxd2	Nc3+
3	Kc1	Be3
4	Bd6	Ke6

Ready to meet the attack on the Knight (5 Bd4) by 5 . . . Nxa2+, winning the rash Bishop.

5	Bf8	Kf6
6	Bd6	Ke6
7	Bf8	d5
8	Ba3	Ke5
9	Bb2	d4

Ready to meet 10 Bxc3 with 10 . . . dxc3, winning the pinned Knight.

continued

10	a3	Kf4
11	Ba1!	Kg3
12	Kb2!	Bxd2
	Stalemate.	

Peronace, 1904

White to play and draw

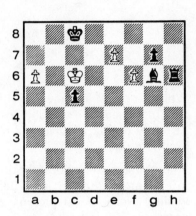

A lovely creation by Peronace, who achieves two stalemate effects—one at the edge of the board and the other in the middle.

	1	a7	Be8 +

Or 1 . . . Be4 + 2 Kd6 Rxf6 + 3 Ke5 Kd7 4 e8 = Q + Kxe8 5 a8 = Q + Bxa8, and White is stalemated.

2	Kb6	Rxf6 +
3	Ka5	Kb7
4	a8 = Q +	Kxa8
	Stalemate.	

Petrov, 1958
White to play and win

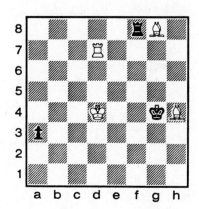

White's combination forces the enemy Rook into a pin. The Rook's only consolation is that he can choose on which square to be pinned!

Black is behind on material, but he threatens to capture one of the Bishops.

1   Rd8!

Parries both threats. Now if 1 . . . Rxd8 2 Bxd8 wins easily, while 1 . . . Kxh4   2 Bxf8 is unthinkable.

So Black concocts a little scheme which will let him threaten both Bishops again.

1	. . .	a2
2	Bxa2	Rf4 +
3	Ke3	Ra4

Now how does White save his Bishops?

4   Bb3   Rb4

Stronger than 4 . . . Ra3, when 5 Rd4 + followed by 6 Rb4 removes all danger.

5   Rd4 + !

continued

A surprise, as the exchange 5 . . . Rxd4 6 Kxd4 Kxh4 lets Black gets away with a draw.

5	. . .	Rxd4
6	Be7!	

A beautiful zwischenzug, which restricts the attacked Rook to one square of the board!

6	. . .	Rf4
7	Be6 +	

Now if 7 . . . Rf5, 8 Ke4 wins the pinned Rook.

7	. . .	Kg3
8	Bd6	

White wins.

The pinned Rook is helpless against the double attack.

ENDING **144**

Pogosyants, 1962
White to play and win

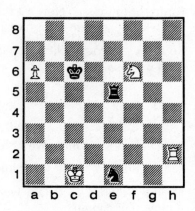

A lovely twist on an original idea of Réti's.

    1   Ra2

Supports the Pawn, and threatens to advance it to the eighth square.

| 1 | ... | Nd3 + |
| 2 | Kd2 | |

Ready to meet 2 . . . Nb4 with 3 a7.

| 2 | ... | Re2 + |

A clever defense. Black sacrifices a Rook, regains it, and is ready to stop the Pawn with his King.

3	Kxe2	Nc1 +
4	Kd2	Nxa2
5	Nd5!	

Beautiful! Black's Knight may not move on pain of capture, while his King must move, but away from the Pawn!

| 5 | ... | Kxd5 |

As good as any.

| 6 | a7 | |
| | **White wins.** | |

Pogosyants, 1967

White to play and win

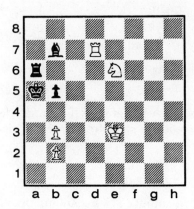

The modest little Pawn at b2 turns out to be the chief actor in this little drama.

| 1 | Nc5 | Bc6 |

Protecting the Bishop by 1 . . . Rb6 or 1 . . . Ra7 does the Bishop no good, since it is attacked by two pieces, while 1 . . . Bc8 loses to 2 b4+ Kb6 3 Rd6+, and after exchanging all the pieces, White has an easily won Pawn ending.

2	Rd6	Rb6
3	b4+	Kxb4
4	Rd4+	Kxc5

Or 4 . . . Ka5

| 5 | b4 mate |

An artistic arrangement.

Prokes, 1941

White to play and draw

That White can force a draw with his Pawns unable to advance to the eighth rank, guarded as it is by a Cerberus of a Rook, is hard to believe.

But White manages it by sacrificing one of his valuable Pawns!

| 1 | Kf4 | Kg7 |
| 2 | a8 = Q! | Rxa8 |

Drawing the Rook away makes it possible for White's King to advance to the center, in accordance with Steinitz's rules for the endgame.

| 3 | Ke5 | Kf7 |
| 4 | Kd6 | Ke8 |

Else 5 Kd7 assures the draw.

| 5 | Kc6 | |

Threatens 6 Kb7, which wins the Rook!

| 5 | ... | Rc8 |
| 6 | Kd6! | |

But not the ambitious 6 Kb7, when 6 . . .   Kd7 wins for Black.

| 6 | ... | Ra8 |
| 7 | Kc6 | |

Drawn by repetition of position.

Prokes, 1944

White to play and win

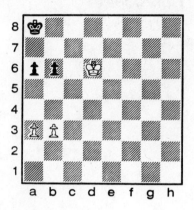

It is not that White's Pawns are stronger than Black's; it's the aggressive position of his King that makes them so.

1	Kc6	Ka7
2	b4	b5

On 2 . . . a5, 3 b5 wins at once.

3	Kc7	a5
4	a4!	

Have your choice!

4	. . .	Ka6

If instead 4 . . . axb4, 5 axb5 b3 6 b6 + wins quickly. Of if 4 . . . bxa4, 5 b5 a3 6 b6 + Ka6 7 b7 a2 8 b8 = Q a1 = Q 9 Qb7 mate.

5	Kc6	axb4

Here if 5 . . . bxa4, 6 b5 + Ka7 7 Kc7.

6	axb5 +	Ka7
7	Kc7	

White wins.

Prokes, 1947

White to play and win

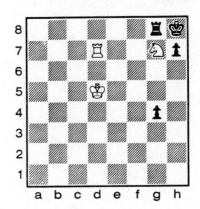

I suppose this finish could qualify as a smothered mate by the Rook.

> **1   Nh5**

Threatens 2 NF6 followed by 3 Rxh7 mate.

> **1   ...**   **Rg5 +**

On 1 . . . Rg6 instead, 2 Ke5 followed by 3 Nf6 wins.

> **2   Ke6**   **Rxh5**
> **3   Kf6**   **h6**

Or 3 . . . Rh6 +, when 4 Kf7 is decisive.

> **4   Kg6**   **Rg5 +**
> **5   Kxh6**   **Rg8**

What else is there?

> **6 Rh7 mate**

Prokes, 1948

White to play and win

A simple but pleasing study. The obvious 1 exf7 gets White nowhere after 1 . . . Bxb3 + followed by 2 . . . Bxf7. No better is 1 e7, which yields to 1 . . . Bxb3 + and 2 . . . Ba4, and the Pawn is halted in its tracks.

1   Ba5 + !

But this changes the complexion of affairs. If now 1 . . . Kxb3, 2 exf7 wins.

1	. . .	Kxa5
2	e7	Bxb3 +
3	Kc5	Ba4
3	b4 mate!	

Proskorovski, 1960

White to play and draw

A duel between the lone King against King, Knight, and Pawn (somewhat like D'Artagnan's duels with the King's guardsmen) results in a surprise stalemate.

1	Kd3	Nc5 +
2	Kc4	Nd7
3	Kd5	Ke7
4	Kc6	Ke6
5	Kb7	Nc5 +
6	Kc6	Nb3
7	Kb6	a5
8	Kb5	Kd5
9	Ka4	Kc4
	Stalemate.	

Réti, 1921

White to play and draw

Réti considered this study of his a trifle. Far from a trifle, it is a masterpiece. In a position where the forces are minimal, White faces what seems to be an insuperable task. He must try to stop a Pawn that appears far out of his reach, and come to the aid of his own Pawn (his only hope), also a good distance away. White's King, in short, must be in two places at once! The solution is a little miracle of ingenuity.

	1	**Kg7**		**h4**

Or 1 . . . Kb6 2 Kf6 Kxc6 (. . . h4 is the game) 3 Kg5 and the Pawn falls.

	2	**Kf6**		**Kb6**

Black plays to kill off a possible threat in White's Pawn. If instead 2 . . . h3, 3 Ke7! h2 4 c7 Kb7 5 Kd7 h1 = Q 6 c8 = Q + and the game is drawn.

	3	**Ke5!**	

Ready to meet 3 . . . Kxc6 with R Kf4, and the Pawn is stopped.

	3	**. . .**		**h3**
	4	**Kd6!**		**h2**
	5	**c7**		

Drawn.

Réti, 1928

White to play and draw

An exquisite miniature (miniature in the number of pieces, not in the concept).

White's task seems insuperable. His King cannot hope to catch the enemy Pawn, since 1 Kf7 is met by 1 . . . g5, and Black wins.

Nor can he threaten to Queen his own Pawn; 1 e7 is thwarted by 1 . . . Bb5.

But there is (as in all Réti compositions) a magic move, which at first sight seems silly.

1   Ke7!!

Blocks the pathway of his own Pawn.

1	. . .	g5
2	Kd6!	g4
3	e7!	Bb5
4	Kc5	

Gains a move by the attack on the Bishop. Now if 4 . . . g3 in reply, 5 Kxb5 draws easily.

| 4 | . . . | Bd7 |
| 5 | Kd4 | |

continued

The King is now close enough to catch the Pawn.

5	...	Kb6
6	Ke3	Kc7
7	Kf4	Kd6
8	e8 = Q	Bxe8
9	Kxg4	

Drawn.

E N D I N G **153**

Réti, 1928

White to play and win

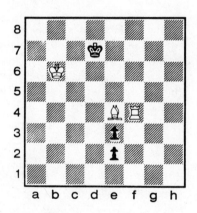

In this miniature, one of Réti's finest creations, the final move is truly brilliant.

1   Bf5 +

The first finesse. If instead 1 Bc6 + Kd6 2 Rd4 + Ke5 3 Re4 + Kd6 4 Rxe3 e1 = Q 5 Rxe1, stalemate!

| 1 | ... | Kd6   (or . . . Kd8) |
| 2 | Rd4 + | Ke7 |

On 2 . . . Ke5 3 Re4 + Kxf5 4 Rxe3 wins.

| 3 | Re5 + | Kd8! |

A subtle defense. On other King moves, the simple 4 Rxe3 wins. Now if 4 Rxe3, there follows 4 . . . e1 = Q 5 Rxe1 and Black is stalemated. But White has a Roland for an Oliver, as the old fiction writers used to say.

4	Bd7!	e1 = Q

Of course 4 . . . Kxd7 is met by 5 Rxe3.

5	Bb5

White wins.

The threat of mate by 6 Re8 can be averted only by 5 . . . Qa5 + , giving up the Queen.

ENDING **154**

Réti, 1929

White to play and draw

Exquisite timing is required to draw this ending. Thoughtless play could lead to zugzwang for White and turn a possible draw into a loss.

1	d6	Ke6
2	d7!	

continued

Gives up a valuable Pawn! The natural 2 Ka7 leads to loss by 2 . . . Bc8 3 Kb8 (on 3 d7, Bxd7 wins) Kd7, and White loses by zugzwang. Thus: 4 Ka7 Kxd6 5 Kb8 Bxg4.

2	. . .	Kxd7
3	Ka7	Bc8

On 3 . . . Be2, 4 Kb8 (or 4 Kb7 Ba6+ 5 Kxa6! draws) Ba6 5 Ka7 etc. draws.

4 Kb8

Now Black is in zugzwang.

4	. . .	Ba6
5	Ka7	
	Drawn.	

If Black continues by 5 . . . Kxc7, then 6 Kxa6 Kd6 7 Kb5 Ke5 8 Kc4 Kf4 9 Kd3 Kxg4 10 Ke2 Kg3 11 Kf1 Kh2 12 Kf2 is convincing enough.

ENDING *155*

Richter, 1954, First Prize
White to play and win

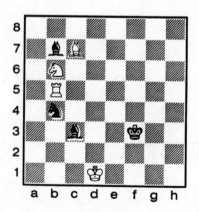

A weird Pawnless position in which the possibilities for attack and counterattack would drive mad a player who tried to analyze the various complications.

1 Na4

White attacks two pieces simultaneously.

1	. . .	**Bc6**
2	**Rf5 +**	**Ke4**

Now it's Black who attacks two pieces simultaneously.

3	**Rf4 +**	**Ke3**
4	**Nxc3**	**Bf3 +**

Forces White into a Knight fork.

5	**Kc1!**	**Nd3 +**
6	**Kc2**	**Nxf4**

Regains the Rook, but . . .

7 Bb6 mate

. . . loses the King.

Rinck, 1905
White to play and win

One of the many beautiful endings that Rinck composed on the theme of Queen and minor piece against Queen is this, where clever play forces Black to choose between losing his Queen or his King.

1   Ng2

Prevents 1 . . . f1 = Q, when 2 Ne3 + ends the short life of the Queen.

1   . . .   Kd2

Comes to the aid of the Pawn, which now threatens to promote to a Queen.

2	a8 = Q	f1 = Q
3	Qa2 +	Kc3

Any other move loses the Queen at once by a Queen check or a Knight fork.

4   Qa3 +   Kd4

Forced, since after 4 . . . Kd2, 5 Qb2 + forces either 5 . . . Kd3, which runs into 6 Qb5 +, or 5 . . . Kd1, which loses by 6 Ne3 +.

5   Qc5 +   Ke4

Once again, 5 . . . Kd3 meets with 6 Qb5 + and loss of the Queen.

But this is worse!

6   Qd5 mate!

ENDING *157*

Rinck, 1907
White to play and win

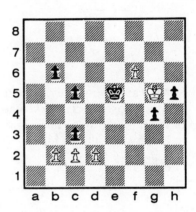

As somebody once said, "Black was lucky to have been mated, or else he would have lost his Queen next move."

1	f7	cxb2
2	f8 = Q	b1 = Q
3	Qe7 +	Kd4
4	Qd7 +	Ke5

On 4 . . . Kc4 instead, 5 Qd3 + Kb4 6 c3 + wins the Queen. Or if 4 . . . Ke4, 5 Qf5 + Kd4 6 c3 + does likewise.

5	c4	

Threat: 6 Qd5 mate.

5	. . .	Qh1
6	d4 +	cxd4
7	Qe7 mate	

Rinck, 1916, First Prize

White to play and draw

Rinck was a miracle worker! In the short space of five moves, White, whose pieces are so widely scattered, gives up nearly all of them (and throws in an underpromotion for good measure) to arrive at an almost incredible draw by stalemate!

1 Kb7!

Threatens mate on the move by 2 Ra4+.

1 . . .   **Bxd1**

But not 1 . . . c4 2 Rxc4 Bxd1 3 Ra4+ Bxa4 4 b4 mate.

2 Ra4+

But not the attractive 2 a8=Q+ Na7 and Black wins (3 b4+ cxb4 4 Rf4 Bb3 and the threat of 5 . . . Bd5 mate is decisive).

2 . . .	**Bxa4**
3 b4+	**cxb4**
4 Qd8+	**Rxd8**
5 a8=B!	

But not 5 a8=Q+ Na7, and Black wins.

Stalemate.

There is no way the King may be allowed a move, nor may the imprisoned Bishop be freed.

Rinck, 1929

White to play and win

Apparently White's passed Pawns can easily be restrained by the Rooks, but three moves are all that are needed to leave Black helpless.

1	h7	Rh1
2	a7	Ra1
3	Rd1!	

And pauses for a reply!

White wins.

Black is faced with an insoluble problem (the hardest kind to handle). To begin with, he is threatened with 4 Rxa1 or 4 Rxh1. Black can avoid this by 3 . . . Rhxd1, but then 4 h8 = Q wins, while on 3 . . . Raxd1, the reply 4 a8 = Q + wins.

Rudenko, 1958

White to play and win

After a lively duel between the Knight and a fleet-footed Queen who manages to cover every mating threat by the Pawns on the seventh, it is a quiet little Pawn move that enables the Knight to inflict mate.

1	e7	Qa4

With this, and the next few moves, Black's Queen covers e8 and a8, the two squares on which White's Pawns threaten to become Queens.

2	Na5	Qe4
3	Nb7	Qa4
4	Nc5	Qc6
5	Nd7	Qe4
6	Ne5	Qa4

So far the Queen has managed to guard ingeniously against White's Queening threats, but now White throws a monkey wrench into the machinery.

7	f7!	

Threatens three mates, of which only two can be averted.

7	...	Bxe7
8	Nxg6 mate	

Runquist, 1962

White to play and win

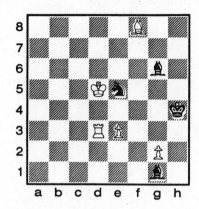

Mate by a pawn is always attractive, whether in the corner of the board or in the center.

| 1 | Rd1 | Bh2 |

The Knight needs protection.

| 2 | Be7 + | Kg4 |

The alternative is 2 . . . Kh5 3 Rh1 Ng4 4 Bd6 Be4 + 5 Kxe4 Nf2 + 6 Kf3 Nxh1 7 Bxh2, and the Knight does not get out alive.

| 3 | Rd4 + | Kf5 |

The choice is limited, as 3 . . . Kg3 loses the Knight, while 3 . . . Kh5 allows mate on the move.

4	g4 +	Nxg4
5	Rf4 +	Bxf4
6	e4 mate	

Sadykov, 1967

White to play and draw

This is one of those unusual endings where the saving device when it comes is almost unbelievable in its suddenness and effect.

1	h7	Nf6
2	h8 = Q	Rb8 +
3	Kd7	Nd5 +
4	Kd6	Rxh8

Obviously Black has no time to take the Rook.

5	Rd4 +	Kd3
6	Ra4	Rd8 +

This saves one of the Knights.

7	Ke5	Nb3 (or ... Nc2)

Now the other Knight is out of danger.

8	Rd4 +!	Nxd4
	Stalemate.	

Sakhodyakin, 1931

White to play and win

White concocts a brilliant finish—an epaulet mate with the Knights settled on the King's shoulders.

1	h6	Ng4 +
2	Kf4	Nxh6

The capture of the Pawn opens a file for White's eager Rook.

3	Kg5	Ng8
4	Rh2 +	Kg7
5	Rh7 +	Kf8 mate
6	Rf7 mate	

Sakhodyakin, 1949

White to play and draw

"Frustration" might be said to be the theme of this ending.

1 Rc7

The tempting 1 Rxe7 + Kf6 2 Rc7 (but not 2 Re1 Rb1) fails after 2 . . . Rb8 + followed by 3 . . . Rb7.

1 . . .	Rb8 +
2 Kxe7	Rb7
3 Rxb7	

Initiates a brilliant little combination.

3 . . .	c1 = Q
4 Ke6 +	Kg6

Of course 4 . . . Kf8 leads nowhere after 5 Rb8 + Ke7 6 Rb7 + .

5 h5 +	Kxh5

On 5 . . . Kg5, 6 Rg7 + forces Black to take the Pawn.

6 Rg7
             Drawn!

Black cannot release his King. If for example 6 . . . Qf1, the reply 7 Ke7 prevents 7 . . . Qf8, and Black can do nothing to force matters.

Sakhodyakin, 1963

White to play and draw

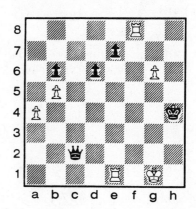

Knight and Pawn maneuver cleverly to squeeze out a draw in this little episode.

1 Ne7 +

White is not tempted by the b-Pawn. It's the advanced h-Pawn that is dangerous.

1 . . .   Ke4

The King moves closer to aid his Pawn by holding back the Knight. Naturally he avoids the squares d6, e5, or d4, which would allow the Pawn to be impaled on a Knight fork.

2 d3 +   Kf3

Here 2 . . . Kxd3 would be met by 3 Ng6 h3 4 Nf4 +, and the Pawn falls.

3 d4   h3

No good comes of 3 . . . Ke4 4 d5 Ke5 5 Ng6 +.

4	**d5**	**h2**
5	**d6**	**h1 = Q**
6	**d7**	**Qh2 +**
7	**Kb3**	**Qd6**

continued

Stops the Pawn from advancing, but White has a cute saving move.

8 Nc6!

Threatens to Queen the Pawn if the Knight is taken, while 8 . . . Qxd7 is neatly met by 9 Ne5 + , winning the Queen.

Drawn.

ENDING **166**

Sakhodyakin, 1967

White to play and win

The key to the win is to render the Queen *hors de combat* in rather original style.

| 1 | g7 | Qg6 + |

The Pawn must be disposed of in a hurry.

| 2 | Kh1 | Qxg7 |
| 3 | Rf4 + | Kh5 |

On 3 . . . Kh3, 4 Re3 + ends the affair.

4	Rf5 +	Kh6 (or . . . Kh4)
5	R1e5!	dxe5
6	Rf2	

Black is helpless against the threat of check on the Rook file and then the Knight file.

6	...	e4
7	Rh2+	Kg5
8	Rg2+	Kf6
9	Rxg7	Kxg7
10	a5	

White wins.

ENDING *167*

Sarychev
White to play and draw

After some elegant fencing between Bishops and Knights, White engineers a finale which is simply amazing. This is as remarkable a finish as I have ever seen!

1 Be3

Attacks one Knight, and threatens to check at d4 and win the other.

| 1 | ... | Nd3+ |
| 2 | Kc3 | Ne1 |

continued

On 2 . . . Nb2 instead, 3 Bc1 wins the Knight.

3	Bd4	Nf5
4	Bf2	Nf3

If 4 . . . Ng7, 5 Bc2 Nfe3 6 Bxe3 Nxe3 7 Bxh7, and the game is drawn.

5	Bc2	Nd6

Black's idea is to win one of the pesky Bishops.

6	Bxh7	Ng5

Intending on a move of White's Bishop, 7 . . .   Ne4+ (either one), which would win a piece and the game.

7	Bc5

Meets the attack with counterattack.

7	. . .	Nb7

It looks as though White must lose a piece.

8	Be7!	Nxh7
9	Kb4	
	Drawn!	

Black's pieces are paralyzed, and all he can do is wait while the enemy King moves up the board to a7 and eats up the Bishop.

Sarychev, 1930

White to play and win

An attractive miniature, in which Black is mated in the middle of the board, just when his Knight is about to make his escape.

1	Ne5	Kg7

Rushes to the aid of his imprisoned Knight.

2	Bd8	

Prevents the King from occupying the central square f6.

2	...	Kf8

Intending to move on to e8.

3	Kf2	Ke8
4	Ba5	Ke7
5	Ke3	Kd6
6	Kd4	Nc7

The Knight finally gets back in play—but at great cost.

7	Bb4 mate!	

Selesniev
White to play and win

White's method is simple. He forces the adverse Rook into one of two plausible defensive moves. Then he attacks the Rook and simultaneously threatens mate, leaving Black helpless to ward off both threats.

1   Kg6

Threatens 2 Kf7, which attacks the Rook and threatens mate at the same time.

1	...	Rxe5
2	Kxf6	Re8
3	Kf7	

White wins.

Should Black at his second move try 2 . . . Rh5, then 3 Kg6 forces the win.

Selesniev, 1913

White to play and win

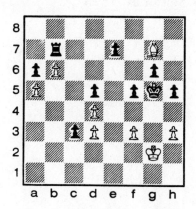

This time the Rook proves no match for the gallivanting Bishop, who roams around the board and forces mate almost single-handedly.

1	f4 + !	Kxf4

Of course not 1 . . . Kh4, when 2 Bh6 followed by 3 Bg5 is mate.

2	Bh6 +	g5
3	Kf2!	

Now the threat is 4 Bg7 followed by 5 Be5 mate.

3	. . .	e5
4	Bf8	

Intending the deadly 5 Ba3 and 6 Bc1 mate.

4	. . .	Rd7
5	Ba3	exd4

Creates a flight square for the King.

6	b7	

Lures the Rook away.

6	. . .	Rxb7
7	Bd6 mate	

Selesniev, 1915

White to play and draw

When all seems hopeless, White saves the situation by cleverly creating a perpetual check.

1	Nc4		Rc5

Attacks the Knight and also prepares to defend by returning to the first rank. The alternative 1 . . . Rd5 would succumb to 2 e7.

2	e7		Rc8
3	Nd6!		

But not 3 g6 fxg6 4 Nd6 Kg8 5 Nxc8 Kf7 and Black wins.

3	. . .		Rg8!

On 3 . . . Rd8 (or 3 . . . Ra8) 4 Nxf7 + Kg8 5 Nd8 wins at once.

4	g6!		fxg6

Forces, as 4 . . . f6 (or 4 . . . f5) allows 5 Nf7 mate.

5	Nf7 +		Kh7
6	Ng5 +		Kh6
7	Nf7 +		Kh7

But not 7 . . . Kh5 8 g4 mate.

8	Ng5 +		Kh6

And so on, far into the night.

Drawn by repetition of position.

Selesniev, 1921
White to play and win

Selesniev considered this one of his finest compositions, in view of the scanty material and the six Pawn checks in succession. Tripled Pawns are usually weak, but this time the column proves irresistible!

1 e4 + !

The obvious 1 Bxd5 loses after 1 . . . fxg3.

1	**. . .**	**Kxe4**
2	**exf3 +**	**Ke5**

But not 2 . . . Kxf3 3 Bxd5 + with an easy win.

3	**gxf4 +**	**Ke6**
4	**f5 +**	**Ke5**
5	**f4 +**	**Ke4**
6	**f3 +**	

White wins.

The King must abandon the Rook, and if 6 . . . Kxf4, 7 Bxd5 h5 8 Kd2 h4 9 Ke2 h3 10 Kf2, and the Pawn is halted.

Selesniev, 1927

White to play and win

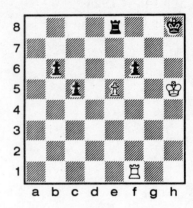

Selesniev could create little miracles out of deceptively simple positions.

1 exf6

Initiates a powerful threat: 2 f7 Rf8 3 Kg6 and White wins easily.

1 ...	Kh7
2 Kg5	

Now the threat is 3 f7 Rf8 (or . . . Re5+) 4 Kf6 and White wins.

2 ...	Re5 +
3 Kf4	Rh5
4 f7	Kg7
5 f8 = Q +	Kxf8
6 Kg4 +	K moves
7 Kxh5	

White wins.

If Black at his third move tries 3 . . . Rd5, then 4 f7 Kg7 5 f8 = Q + Kxf8 6 Ke4 + forces the win.

Sobalevski, 1951

White to play and win

This would seem to be a difficult position to analyze, with so many pieces being en prise.

1	Nh8+!	Kg8
2	Kxg2	

The alternative 2 Kxh2 would be met by 2 . . . Ne3, threatening 3 . . . Ng4+ as well as the simple 3 . . . Kxh8.

2	. . .	Bf4

Prevents 3 Ng5, when 3 . . . Bxg5 draws for Black.

3	Ng6	Bh6
4	Ng5	Bg7!

Clever defense! On 5 Bd8 in reply there follows 5 . . . Bf6 6 Ne7+ (but not 6 Bxf6, stalemate) Kf8 7 Nh7+ Ke8, and the game is drawn.

5	Ne7+	Kh8

But not 5 . . . Kf8 6 Ne6+.

6	Nf7+	

Remarkable maneuvering at close quarters.

6	. . .	Kh7
7	Bh4	Bf6!

continued

Ingenious to the last! If 8 Bxf6 Black is stalemated.

8	Ng5 +	Kh6
9	Ng8 +	Kh5
10	Nxf6 +	Kxh4
11	Nf3 mate	

A marvelous production.

Stodenetzky, 1962
White to play and win

Black meets checkmate at every turn. It's enough to discourage a King!

1	h6!	gxh6

Black's best chance. If instead 1 . . . g5 2 c5 d4 3 c6 d3 4 c7 d2 5 c8 = Q d1 = ! 6 Qh3mate.

Or if 1 . . . g6 2 g3+ Kg5 (taking the g-Pawn would let White play 3 cxb5 and Queen with check) 3 cxb5 d4 4 b6 d3 5 b7 d2 6 b8 = Q d1 = Q 7 Qf4+ Kh5 8 Qh4 mate.

Finally, if 1 . . . g6 2 g3+ Kh5 3 c5! b4 4 c6 b3 5 c7 b2 6 c8 = Q b1 = Q 7 Qh3+ Kg5 8 Qh4+ Kf5 9 Qf4 mate.

2	g3+	Kg5

Or 2 . . . Kh5 3 c5 b4 4 c6 b3 5 c7 b2 6 c8 = Q b1 = Q 7 Qh3 + Kg5
8 Qh4 + Kf5 9 Qf4 + Kg6 10 Qg4 mate.

3	cxb5	d4
4	b6	d3
5	b7	d2
6	b8 = Q	d1 = Q
7	Qf4 +	Kg6
8	Qf6 +	Kh5
9	Qf5 mate	

Strycek, 1967, First Prize

White to play and win

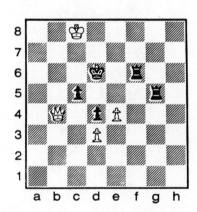

No matter how Black captures a Pawn that is offered, it leads to
a mate where his King's exit is blocked by the Rooks.

1	e5 +	Kxe5

If 1 . . . Rxe5, 2 Qb6 + Ke7 3 Qc7 + Ke6 4 Qd7 mate.

2	Qxc5 +	Kf4
3	Qxd4 +	Kf5
4	Qe4 mate	

Szental, 1966

White to play and win

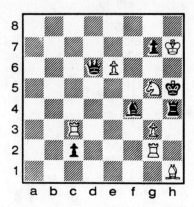

White forces Black's pieces to huddle about the King, whom he then polishes off with a spin mate.

1   Ne4

Other possibilities are 1 gxf4 Rxh1, and Black should win, or 1 gxh4 c1 = Q 2 Rxc1 Bxc1, and again Black should win.

After the actual move White threatens 2 g4 + Rxg4 3 Rh3 + Rh4 4 Rg5 + Bxg5 5 Bf3 mate.

| 1 | . . . | Qxe6 |
| 2 | g4 + | Rxg4 |

Or 2 . . . Qxg4 3 Rc5 + g5 4 Nf6 mate.

3	Rh3 +	Rh4
4	Rg5 +	Bxg5
5	Bf3 +	Qg4
6	Ng3 mate	

How embarrassing!

Szijarov, 1957

White to play and win

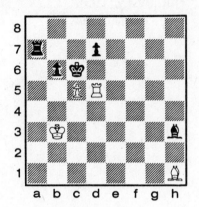

White weaves an artful mating net about the King.

1	Rd6 + +	Kb5

Immediate loss follows 1 . . . Kc7, by 2 cxb6 + Kxd6 3 bxa7, and White gets a new Queen and wins.

2	cxb6	Be6 +
3	Rxe6	Rb7

Ingenious, as after 4 Bxb7 dxe6 the Pawn falls.

4	Re5 +	d5
5	Bxd5	Rxb6
6	Bb7 mate	

ENDING *179*

Tjaulovsky, 1959

White to play and win

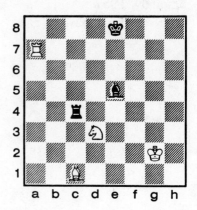

Checkmate on an open board is the last thing you would look for in this miniature study.

| 1 | Ra8 + | | Ke7 |

Moving to a white square allows 2 Nxe5 + , winning Rook and Bishop.

| 2 | Bg5 + | | Bf6 |

Again, there is no choice; 2 . . . Ke6 loses to 3 Re8 + , as does 2 . . . Kd6 to 3 Ra6 + Kd5 4 Ra5 + , in each case winning the Bishop.

3	Ra7 +		Ke6
4	Ra6 +		Kf5
5	Bxf6		Rg4 +
6	Kf3		Rg6

Pins and hopes to win the Bishop.

| 7 | Nf4 | | Rxf6 |

Regains his piece—but loses his King!

| 8 | Ra5! mate |

ENDING *180*

Tresovski, 1960

White to play and draw

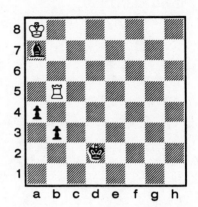

Quite in the classic style of Kubbel, this ending is simple and elegant.

1   Rb4

Capturing the Bishop is fatal, as the reply 1 . . . Kc2 assures the Queening of one of the Pawns.

1   ...   Kc3

On 1 . . . Bc5 2 Rxa4 b2 3 Ra2 followed by removing the Pawn draws.

2	Rxa4	b2
3	Ra3+	Kc4
4	Ra4+	Kc5

Clearly on 4 . . . Kb5, 5 Rxa7 draws easily.

5	Ra5+	Kc6
6	Ra1!	bxa1 = Q

Stalemate.

Tresovski, 1960

White to play and win

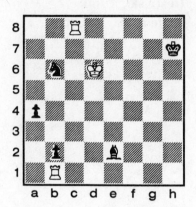

White meets the threat of the united passed Pawns by weaving a mating net on the other side of the board!

| 1 | Rc6 | Nc4 + |

On 1 . . . a3, the continuation 2 Rxb6 a2 3 Rh1+ Kg7 4 Rxb2 wins for White.

2	Ke7	Bd3
3	Rh1 +	Kg7
4	Rg1 +	Kh7
5	Kf8	

Threatens 6 Rh1 mate.

5	. . .	b1 = Q
6	Rg7 +	Kh8
7	Rh6 +	Bh7
8	Rg8 mate	

(Note that neither 8 Rhxh7+ nor 8 Rgxh7+ is mate.)

Troitzky

White to play and win

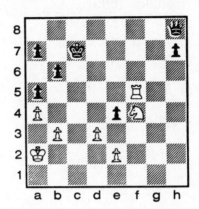

An attractive study in which the Queen proves no match for the Knight, who dominates the proceedings.

1	Rf8!	Qe5

The only square on the board on which the Queen does not fall onto a Knight fork.

Now the Queen is centralized—but still in danger for her life.

2	d4!	Qd6

Once again, only one square offers safety.

3	Rf6!	Qd7

For the third time, the Queen is restricted to one square!

4	Ne6 +	Kb8 (or . . . Kc8)

Moving to the third rank instead allows a discovered check, winning the Queen.

5	Rf8 +	Kb7
6	Rf7!	Qxf7
7	Nd8 +	

White wins.

The Queen falls, and with it the game.

Troitzky, 1895

White to play and win

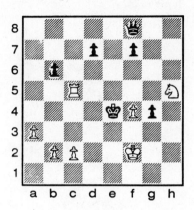

Troitzky is an artist who needs a minimum of material to create a masterpiece.

An interesting feature of this composition is the way threats of Knight forks on white squares suddenly transform into threats of Knight forks on black squares. This little beauty is one of my favorite Troitzky studies.

 1 Ng3 +   **Kd4**

Obviously 1 . . . Kxf4 2 Rf5 mate.

 2 Rc8!   **Qxc8**

If she moves along either of the two diagonals, she falls onto a Knight fork at f5.

 3 Nf5 +   **Kc5**

Moving to a white square loses the Queen by a Knight fork.

 4 b4 +

Bayonet attack!

     White wins.

The King must move to a white square—and lose the Queen by a Knight fork, thus 4 . . . Kc6 5 Ne7 + ; or 4 . . . Kb5 5 Nd6 + ; or 4 . . . Kd5 5 Ne7 + ; or 4 . . . Kc4 5 Nd6 + .

Troitzky, 1897
White to play and win

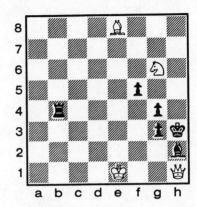

A neat smothered mate, which Troitzky himself called "a romantic study."

White is ahead in material, but he is threatened with loss of the Queen by 1 . . . g2, as well as by 1 . . . Rb1 + .

(Luckily, it's his turn to move.)

1 Bc6!

A clever combination, including as it does a sacrifice of the Queen. . .

1	. . .	Rb1 +
2	Ke2	Rxh1
3	Bg2 +!	

. . . and a sacrifice of the Bishop!

3	. . .	Kxg2
4	Nf4 +	Kg1
5	Ke1	g2
6	Ne2 mate	

Troitzky, 1898

White to play and win

White's pieces work beautifully together to subdue the enemy King. A simple but artistic production.

1   Nh6

Threatens instant mate.

1   . . .   Bf8

Black may not move the King, on pain of a Knight fork.

2	Bf6+	Bg7
3	Ke5!	c5
4	Ke6	c4
5	Kf7	Bxf6
6	Kxf6	c3
7	Kf7	c2
8	Kf8	c1 = Q
9	Nf7 mate	

Troitzky, 1909
White to play and win

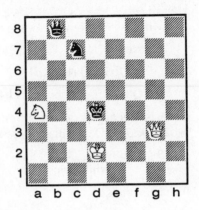

A classic production of the old master.

    1   Nb6!

With the immediate threat of mate by 2 Qe3.

    1   ...   Qe8

The King may not move, on pain of losing the Queen.

    2   Nd7!

With a new mate threat—3 Qd3.

    2   ...   Kc4

The King may not move to any other square, or he will lose his Queen. And if 2 . . . Qe4, 3 Qc3 + Kd5 4 Nf6 + wins the Queen.

    3   Qxc7 +   Kb4
    4   Qc5 +   Kb3

On 4 . . . Ka4 White forces matters by 5 Nb6 + Kb3 6 Qc3 + Ka2 7 Nd5! Qd7 8 Kc1.

    5   Qc3 +   Ka4

Or 5 . . . Ka2 6 Kc1 Qe2 7 Qa5 + Kb3 8 Nc5 + Kc4 9 Qa6 + and Black's Queen falls.

continued

6   Qd4 +   **Ka3**

Here if 6 . . . Kb5 7 Qc5 + Ka4 8 Nb6 + Kb3 9 Qc3 + Ka2 10 Nd5
and wins, as in the note to Black's 4th move.

7   Nc5   **Qb8**

On 7 . . . Qb5 8 Qa1 + Kb4 9 Qc3 is mate.

8   Qa1 +   **Kb4**

Care is necessary when administering the final touch. If 9
Qb2 + Ka5 10 Qxb8, Black escapes by stalemate.

9   Na6 +
        White wins.

A masterpiece!

E N D I N G *187*

Troitzky, 1917
White to play and win

Queen and Knight cooperate beautifully to win the enemy
Queen by "domination."

1   Qa3 +   **Kd2**

Safe temporarily, but the King will be forced to move to c2.

2	Qa5 +		Kc2

Forced, since 2 . . . Kd3 loses to 3 Qa6 + , 2 . . . Ke2 loses to 3 Ng3 + , 2 . . . Kc1 loses to 3 Qa1 + , and 2 . . . Kd1 loses to 3 Qa1 + Ke2 4 Ng3 + .

3	Qa2 +		Kc3

Obviously the only move left.

4	Ng3

Domination!

4	. . .		Qf8

On 4 . . . Qd1 5 Ne4 + forces the King into a Knight fork.

5	Ne4 +	Kd3
6	Qd2 +	Kxe4
7	Qe2 +	

White wins.

The King must move to the Bishop file, when 8 Qf2 + wins the Queen.

Troitzky, 1929

White to play and draw

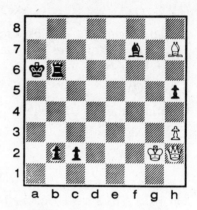

The situation looks desperate for White. Though he is ahead in material, his opponent has two Pawns on the second rank, ready to promote to Queens.

1 Bd3 + !

The natural 1 Bxc2 fails after 1 . . . b1 = Q 2 Bxb1 Rb2 + 3 Kg3 (or Kg1 Rxb1 + 4 Kf2 Rb2 + 5 Kg3 Rxh2 and Black wins) 3 . . . h4 +, and Black wins the Queen.

1 . . .   Kb7

The King does not care to be disturbed by checks.

2	Bxc2	b1 = Q
3	Bxb1	Rb2 +
4	Kg3!	h4 +
5	Kxh4	Rxh2
6	Be4 +	K moves
7	Bg2!	

Confines the Rook and threatens to win it by 8 Kg3.

7 . . .   Rxg2
                 Stalemate.

Troitzky, 1930

White to play and win

Wherein a piece may seem to have freedom of movement, and yet be hopelessly trapped.

1	Rg4 +		Kh8

The King must go to the Rook file, since moving to the Bishop file allows 2 Rc4 +, winning a Bishop.

2	c7	Bf5
3	Rf4	Bb3

Black is willing to give up a Bishop, if he can thereby remove the dangerous Pawn.

4	Rxf5	Bxc7
5	Kc6	

White wins.

To Black's surprise, the Bishop does not have a decent move left. If 5 . . . Bg3, 6 Rh5 + Kg7 7 Rg5 + and the Bishop falls.

Troitzky, 1935

White to play and win

After two forceful checks, a quiet move by the King places Black in zugzwang—any move he makes leads to disaster.

A typical Troitzky masterpiece.

1   Qf7 +   Kc3

Best, as 1 . . . Ka4 allows 2 Qc4 + and mate at b4.

2   Bxg7 +   Kd3

The only move, as 2 . . . Kb4 loses the Queen after 3 Bf8 + .

3   Kd1!

After this quiet move, Black is left without a single tenable reply; none of his pieces may move without loss.

For example: if 3 . . . Ke4, 4 Qb7 + , and the King may not go to a black square on account of a Bishop check exposing his Queen, while moving to a white square is met by 4 Qb1 + , which wins the Queen by the skewer attack.

If 3 . . . Qh2, 4 Qd5 + Ke3 5 Bd4 + ; or if 3 . . . Qh4 (or 3 . . . Qh1), 4 Qb3 + , and the Queen goes.

Finally, if 3 . . . Ng2, 4 Qb3 + wins the Queen, while 3 . . . Nc2 4 Qb3 + Ke4 5 Qxc2 + does likewise.

3	...	a5
4	Qb3 +	Ke4
5	Qb7 +	
	White wins.	

This long-distance check finally wins the Queen. A King move to a white square succumbs to 6 Qb1 +, while a move to a black square is met by 6 Be5 + or 6 Bd4 +, and the Queen falls.

ENDING **191**

Unknown
White to play and draw

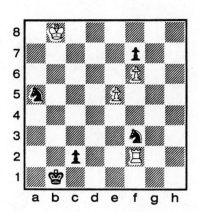

There is some clever footwork by the Knights in this ending.

1	Rf1 +	c1 = Q
2	Rxc1 +	Kxc1
3	e6	fxe6
4	f7	Ne5

Attacks the Pawn and threatens, if it Queens, to win the Queen by 5 . . . Nd7 +.

5	f8 = N	

continued

If White can win the Pawn, even at the cost of his Knight, he will draw, since two lone Knights cannot force mate.

5	...	Nec6+
6	Ka8	e5
7	Nd7	e4
8	Nf6	e3
9	Nd5	e2
10	Nf4	

Duplicates Black's earlier threat! He attacks the Queening Pawn in the same fashion.

10	...	e1 = N
11	Nd3 +	Nxd3
	Stalemate!	

ENDING *192*

Vandecasteele, 1967
White to play and win

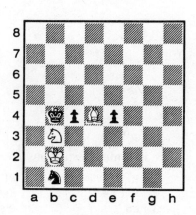

The minor-piece play is exquisite—a masterpiece if I ever saw one.

1	Nc1	Na3

The only move, since 1 . . . Nd2 allows 2 Bc3 + .

2	Na2+	Ka4
3	Nc3+	Kb4
4	Nd5+	Ka4
5	Nb6+	

The tempting 5 Bc3 allows Black a beautiful escape: 5 . . . e3 6 Be1 e2 7 Nc3+ Kb4 8 Nb1+ c3+ 9 Bxc3+ Ka4 10 Nxa3 e1 = Q 11 Bxe1 stalemate!

5	. . .	Kb4

On 6 . . . Kc5, 7 Na4+ wins the Black Knight.

7	Nd7	Ka4

Of course 7 . . . Kc6 loses a piece to 8 Ne5+.

8	Nc5+	Kb5
9	Nxe4	Ka4

Black's Knight is curiously helpless to escape.

10	Nc5+	Kb5
11	Nd7	Ka4

Here too 11 . . . Kc6 fails after 12 Ne5+.

12	Nb6+	Kb5
13	Bd4	Kb4
14	Nd5+	Ka4
15	Bc3	Nb5

Finally the Knight is able to make away—but alas! It's too late.

16	Nb6 mate	

ENDING **193**

Villaneuve-Escaplon, 1910
Either Bishop to play and win

That the advantage of being "on the move" can offer winning chances is nicely illustrated in this ending.

White moves first:

| 1 | Bh5 | Kxh5 |

Running away loses: 1 Kg7 2 Qg6 + Kh8 3 Qf6 + Kg8 (on 3 . . . Kh7, 4 Bg6 + wins) 4 Bf7 + Kf8 5 Bg6 + and mate in two.

2	Qh7 +	Kg5
3	Qh3 +	Kf3
4	Qg2 +	

White wins the Queen.
Black moves first:

1	. . .	Bh3
2	Kxh3	Qh1 +
3	Kg4	Qh4 +
4	Kf5	Qg6 +

Black wins the Queen and the game.

ENDING *194*

Voia, 1957

White to play and draw

Both Kings race madly down the board, Black's to win the Knight, White's to rescue it. In this wide-open position, a draw by stalemate seems rather unlikely.

1	Ne4	h2
2	Ng3	

There's not time to take the Bishop; the Pawn must be stopped.

2	. . .	Bd6
3	Nh1	Kb6
4	Kf7	Kc5
5	Ke6!	Bc7

An unfortunate necessity. If Black tries to gain time by abandoning the Bishop, this might happen: 5 . . . Kd4 6 Kxd6 Ke4 7 Kc5 Kf3 8 Kd4 Kg2 9 Ke3 Kxh1 10 Kf2, stalemate.

6	Kf5	Kd4
7	Kg4	Ke3
8	Kh3	Kf3
9	Ng3!	

The saving move!

9	. . .	Bxg3
	Stalemate.	

Vukevic

White to play and win

White wins the black Queen, then seems in danger of losing his own. He evolves a little combination that ends in as pretty a checkmate as you'll ever see!

1	Rf5 +	Qxf5
2	Ne3 +	Kxd6
3	Nxf5 +	Kc7

How does the white Queen escape? Answer: she doesn't!

4	Qxa7 +	Nxa7
5	b6 +	Kb7
6	Nd6 +	Ka8
7	b7 mate!	

Lovely!

Wotawa

White to play and win

White's strategy is brusque, but effective. He sacrifices both Rooks—offers that cannot be refused. The resulting Queen ending is child's play.

1 Rd2!

Threatens both 2 Rxe2, and 2 Rb2 + with mate to follow. The reply is forced.

1	...	Rxd2
2	Rh1 +	Rd1
3	Re1!	Rxe1

Again there is no choice.

4	e7	Rd1
5	e8 = Q	e1 = Q
6	Qg6 +	Ka1
7	Qf6 +	Kb1
8	Qb2 mate	

Wotawa, 1939

White to play and win

The Rook finds a way to break through against any line of play by the Pawns.

	1	c3!	
(a)	1	...	f2
	2	d3!	cxd3
	3	c4	g3
	4	c5	

Threatens Rb6 mate.

4	...	dxc5
5	Rh1	

And the Rook mates.

(b)	1	...	g3
	2	d3	g2

Or 2 . . . d5 and 3 d4 wins; or if 2 . . . cxd3 3 c4 g2 4 c5 dxc5 5 Re1 wins.

3	dxc4	f2
4	c5	dxc5
5	Rd1	

And mate next move.

(c)	1	...	d5!
	2	Rh1	Kb6

3	Rh6+	Kc5
4	Kc7	

Threatens 5 Rc6 mate.

4	. . .	d4
5	Rh5 mate	

E N D I N G *198*

Wotawa, 1952

White to play and draw

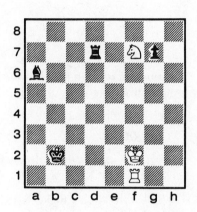

With two pieces en prise, White has his work cut out to emerge with a draw. His method is ingenious.

1	Ne5	Rd2+

On 1 . . . Rd5, 2 Re1 is the simplest way to draw.

2	Ke3	Re2+

The situation looks bad. If now 3 Kf4, Rxe5 4 Rf2+ Re2 5 Rxe2+ Bxe2 6 Kg5 Bd3 wins for Black.

3	Kd4!	Rxe5
4	Rf6!	

White attacks two pieces—but his own Rook is under attack!

4	. . .	gxf6
	Stalemate.	

Wotawa, 1952

White to play and draw

It seems incredible that in four moves White can bring about a stalemate in the middle of the board.

Watch some magic moves by White.

| 1 | Kd4 | Ne7 (or Nf6) |

After 1 . . . Ra5, White draws by 2 Ne1 followed by Nd3 and Nc5.

For example, 1 . . . Ra5 2 Ne1 Kf5 3 Nd3 Ke6 4 Nc5+ Kd6(?) 5 Nb7+.

2	Nc7	Rc6
3	Nd5!	Nxd5
4	Nb4!	Nxb4
	Stalemate.	

ENDING 200

Yakimchik

White to play and win

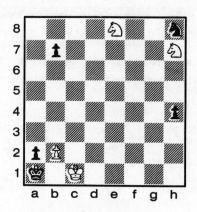

There is some lively steppin' in this Knightly duel.

1   Ng5

Stops the passed Pawn, and also heads for c2 or b3.

1 ...	Ng6
2 Ne6	

Guards f4 against Nf4 and an annoying check next move.

2   ...   Nf4!

With stalemate in mind.

3 Nxf4	h3
4 Nxh3	b5
5 Nf2	b4
6 Nd1	b3

Black seems about to achieve his goal—stalemate.

7 Kd2	Kb1
8 Nd6	

The second Knight decides to take a hand. . .

8 ...	a1 = Q
9 Nc3 +	Kxb2
10 Nc4 mate	

. . . and just in time.